CONVERSIONS, SCRATCHBUILDING, AND SUPERDETAILING

EDITED BY
JASON NICHOLAS MOORE

FONTHILL

www.fonthill.media
office@fonthillmedia.com

First published in the United Kingdom
and the United States of America 2024

British Library Cataloguing in Publication Data:
A catalogue record for this book is available from the British Library

ISBN 978-1-78155-896-6

Typeset in 10.5pt on 13pt Myriad Pro
Printed and bound in England

I dedicate this book to the Frog/Penguin Company, who started it all.

Preface

This book is intended for the average competent modeller: someone who already knows how to build a decent-looking model out of a mainstream kit, but who wishes to do more. It does not delve deeply into the basics of modelling such as detaching parts from sprues, when to use a brush or an airbrush, or how to attach clear parts, etc. It is assumed that the reader already knows these basics. Instead, this book concentrates on more advanced topics like how to make conversions of kits, how to work with resin and vacuform kits, how to scratchbuild entire models, and how to superdetail models. You, the reader, may never attain the levels of proficiency demonstrated by the master modellers in this book, but you will learn techniques that will improve your model-building skills and the look of your model aeroplanes. For example, although most modellers will never scratchbuild an entire model, the skills used in scratchbuilding models will help you to scratchbuild parts for kits.

This book is composed of four sections, each covering a specific modelling technique: namely, how to do conversions, how to build resin and vacuform models, how to scratchbuild models, and how to superdetail models. A model or two (or more) is used to illustrate each of the techniques necessary for modelling these types of kit, and in addition to text outlining the procedures, there are photographs to illustrate the techniques. The text and photographs have been provided by a panel of contributing master modellers.

This book is not intended to be a complete step-by-step how-to guide for the models represented (each one of these models could have had its own book dedicated to it); rather, it is meant more to give you, the reader, some useful pointers and an overall feel for what is involved if you wish to stretch your modelling skills to the next level. If, after reading this book, you feel motivated to tackle some ambitious modelling projects of your own, or to restart a long-abandoned project, then it has fulfilled its purpose.

Acknowledgements

I must first acknowledge the master modellers who contributed examples of their expertise to this book. Obviously without them this book would not have been possible. I would also like to acknowledge the fine modelling site Britmodeller.com, on which some of the models in this book have appeared. As always, I thank Fonthill Media, who continue to turn my rough manuscripts into fine books. Lastly, I thank my family, whose general tolerance over the years of my magnificent obsession with plastic modelling has made this book possible.

Contents

Introduction

Miniature representations of ships, people, and animals were found in the tomb of Pharaoh Tutankhamun (*c.* 1341–1323 BCE), so scale models have been around for a very long time indeed. Modern plastic modelling began, in earnest, with the Frog Company of the United Kingdom, which started producing kits of aeroplanes made from cellulose acetate, an early type of plastic, in 1932. It was Frog and Skybirds, another very early British kit manufacturer, which popularised the now familiar scale of 1/72, meaning the kit was seventy-two times smaller than the original, full-sized example. This is my favourite scale. Models in various scales made from resin were produced during the Second World War as recognition aids and are now collectibles.

It was only after the Second World War, however, in the 1950s, that plastic modelling really began to 'take off' with the introduction of injection-moulded polystyrene plastic as the main medium. Brands such as Revell, Lindbergh, Aurora, Monogram, Airfix, and others appeared, some now long gone in their original form, but some, such as Revell and Airfix, still very much with us in 2023. These early polystyrene kits were often characterised by rather striking box art and 'gimmicky' features such as opening bomb bays and retractable landing gear. Some of the American kits were also characterised by some rather odd scales like 1/130. They were called 'box scales' as the kits were scaled to fit the available boxes, unlike the established scales such as 1/72, which were packaged in boxes made to fit the scale. These models were aimed at a relatively young audience of children and teenagers, and in some cases were little more than semi-scale toys. They often came with multiple working features, which may have added to their attractiveness but did not improve their accuracy.

In the 1960s and 1970s, now-famous Japanese brands such as Fujimi, Hasegawa, and Tamiya became available to 'Western' modellers. These brands introduced features such as engraved panel lines, which are now common. Working features such as opening bomb bay doors and retracting landing gear fell out of fashion. Sadly, it was also during the 1970s that Frog produced their last kits. Monogram in the United States popularised 1/48 scale kits (which they had been producing since the 1950s), which offered better detail than the smaller 1/72 scale kits. Revell (an American company at the time) introduced their 1/32 scale kits in the 1960s. These were the first truly large-scale plastic kits produced in any quantity, offering a level of detail otherwise unknown at the time. Vacuform kits, available since the 1950s, became ubiquitous, offering many large and unusual aircraft. They were popularised by RAREplanes of the United Kingdom, with the kits being designed by the late, great Gordon Stevens.

The 1970s and early 1980s also brought the beginning of limited-run injection-moulded kits, originally as small one-person 'cottage industry' ventures. Previously 'unkitted' aircraft were now available for those with a little (or more than a little) skill in making injection-moulded kits but not interested in either vacuform or resin kits. Unlike mainstream manufacturers, who injected liquid plastic into steel moulds to produce their kits, limited-run manufacturers initially used resin moulds, the plastic being injected often under low pressure and the moulds having limited lifespans. This method is still used by some limited-run manufacturers today. Pegasus in the United Kingdom was one of the pioneers in these types of kits, and their line included everything from First World War aircraft to post-war jets.

Resin kits made from polyurethane resin became more popular and sophisticated in the 1980s and offered aircraft not available in injection-moulded form, or even as vacuforms. These resin and limited-run plastic kits were aimed at a more mature and experienced audience of skilled, adult modellers, with more disposable cash at hand. The limited runs (perhaps as few as 500 kits) demanded a higher cost to recoup the expense for the manufacturers (there was no economy of scale for these types of kits). In addition, they were 'rougher' than mainstream kits, often with heavy 'flash' (plastic which had seeped between the halves of the moulds), and sparser interior and exterior detail.

In the 1990s, the aftermarket business exploded, with photoetched parts, resin detail parts, and decals becoming available for many kits (although aftermarket decal sheets had been available since at least the 1960s). First Verlinden, a Belgian company, now unfortunately gone, then Eduard, a Czech company, still very much extant, appeared with many aftermarket items in both resin and as photoetched parts. The internet also appeared on the scene and offered a new medium by which modelling companies could advertise and sell their wares, and modellers could communicate with each other, sharing their models and techniques on dedicated sites. The 2000s and 2010s saw a shrinkage of the once booming vacuform market, at least partially in response to the expansion of the injection-moulded market, which now covered subjects once only available as vacuform kits. To a great extent, limited-run injection-moulded kits took the place of vacuform kits, although a few vacuform manufacturers, such as the Polish Broplan and Welsh Models, are still around in 2023. The Czech Republic has become a hotbed for limited-run manufacturing, with companies like Special Hobby and Sword producing rather complex and detailed limited-run kits. 1/48 scale kits, with their greater detailing (and scope for detailing), became more and more popular with modellers until, by the end of the 2010s, they seemed to have overtaken 1/72 scale kits in popularity.

Injection-moulded kits have become not only more detailed (both on the interior and the exterior) and more accurate, but they now include subjects that have never before been kitted even in vacuform or resin. The dividing line between the increasingly sophisticated limited-run manufacturers and the mainstream manufacturers has become blurred to the point where it is sometimes hard to tell where one ends and the other begins. No longer are limited-run kits just the province of one-person cottage industry operations using resin moulds; now some are multi-person enterprises using steel moulds like the mainstream manufacturers. Resin kits continue to be manufactured, with a few manufacturers such as Prop & Jet (of Russia) capable of producing kits that, in terms of fineness of moulding and detail, are equal to (or better than) those of most mainstream plastic injection-moulded kit manufacturers.

Few modellers would disagree that the golden age of plastic aeroplane modelling is now upon us. With the advent of 3-D printing and computer-aided design (CAD), the market should continue to grow, and the choice of subjects should continue to expand. LIDAR ('light detection and ranging' or 'laser imaging, detection, and ranging'), a technique that involves lasers measuring with immense accuracy the sizes and shapes of full-sized aircraft, is being used with CAD to create extremely detailed and accurate kits. Completely 3-D printed kits are now available, and I foresee a time in the near future when previously unavailable subjects will be readily available via computer files, with the kits being printed out at home using personal 3-D printers. This process has already begun. We have indeed come a long way since the first crude cellulose acetate kits were produced by Frog in the 1930s.

Jason Nicholas Moore,
Seguin, Texas,
14 January 2024

1
Conversions

Sometimes the aircraft you wish to model is available as a kit, but the particular version you want is not. This is where conversions come in, taking a kit and converting it into a different version of the aircraft, or even a different aircraft. Some conversions can be as simple as adding a new nose or even just new decals, but some are deep conversions, which may involve turning the kit into a different aircraft. The latter is what will be done with the two models in this section.

Many conversion sets are now available, usually in polyurethane resin (sometimes also with metal and photoetched parts), though some sets are still in vacuform. Both types of conversion sets enable the modeller to make the necessary changes to the model, and these sets sometimes even include decals. At times, when the conversion set does not exist, the modeller is then forced to make the conversion himself/herself, utilising aftermarket items such as sheet plastic, plastic rod, and putty. Although more difficult than using 'ready-made' conversion sets, these 'self-made' conversions can be very satisfying, as I can attest to, having converted the 1/72 scale Hasegawa Lockheed P2V-7/ SP-2H Neptune into the earlier P2V-4 variant.

Both of the conversions in this section start out as Avro Lancasters, but different aeroplanes emerge at the end: different from each other, and different from the original donor Lancaster. They show how the same base aircraft kit (or donor) can be converted into two very different aircraft.

1/48 SCALE AVRO MANCHESTER (FROM TAMIYA AVRO LANCASTER)

Before there was the deservedly famous Avro Lancaster, there was the notorious Avro Manchester. Designed to the same specification that led to the successful Handley-Page Halifax four-engined heavy bomber, the Manchester was a heavy bomber powered by two Rolls-Royce Vulture twenty-four-cylinder engines. The engines, essentially two Peregrine engines joined together to drive one propeller shaft, proved to be the weak spot of the Manchester, being unreliable and prone to catching fire. The Manchester was out of service by 1942, but re-engined with four Rolls-Royce Merlin engines, it re-emerged as the excellent Lancaster bomber. The Lancaster went on to serve with distinction throughout the rest of the Second World War and far beyond. The Tamiya 1/48 scale kit of the Lancaster bomber serves as the basis for this conversion.

Avro Manchester 1/48 Scale Resin Conversion Set by Neil Woodall

The Avro Manchester is famous for two things: first, its unreliability, which was due mainly to its underdeveloped Rolls-Royce Vulture engines. On summer evenings with full loads, crews would often take off with sparks coming out of the exhausts and oil temperature gauges in the red. For some, being over Germany must have been less intimidating than simply getting airborne. Such was the pressure of war that the Manchester was needed in service before the bugs were ironed out, and this meant that feedback was flowing constantly between the squadrons, Avro, and Rolls-Royce. It followed that alterations were being carried out all the time, and often literally in the field. This makes it difficult to determine exactly when certain modifications were introduced and to which individual aircraft. The second reason for the Avro Manchester's fame is its daughter, the mighty Lancaster, which evolved from the Manchester design and needs no introduction. Despite its dogged history, the Manchester Mk Ia with twin tall tails is, in my opinion, the most beautiful of the subsequent lineage right up to the Lincoln, although I'm sure this would start an argument with Lancaster fans!

This build was carried out in parallel to the 1/48 scale Lincoln build, again after managing to source a beautiful Paragon Manchester conversion set for a sum that, thankfully, did not require a remortgage. That said, on the bench at the time I had two Tamiya Lancasters and two incredibly rare Paragon conversion sets, so there was still a considerable sum of money invested into what I was about to hack to pieces!

Work started on the interior. The intent was to use the Eduard pre-painted interior etch set for the Lancaster and some additional scratchbuilding to enhance the Tamiya detail offered from the box. The challenge here, however, was that the Manchester had only two engines, so the banks of four gauges on the pilot's instrument panel and engineers' panel were incorrect. To date, I've never seen a photo of the engineer's panel on a Manchester, so I took the simple (if incorrect) route and overpainted the gauges for two of the engines on both panels with matt black.

Unlike the later Lancasters and Lincolns, which had black interiors, early interiors on the Manchester were cockpit green throughout, and while they were both on my expensive production line, the Lincoln and Manchester received similar enhancements. This included the pilot's seat getting additional framework to the base and head armour folding mechanism. Storage boxes to the right of the pilot's seat were also added. The canopy's internal structure was detailed, requiring great care to ensure that the PVA did not run across the windowpanes. Improvements here included a folded-up curtain made from rolled up Blu Tack, along with curtain rails made from stretched sprue. I also added side window handles made from thin brass wire and an interior light.

With the interior largely complete, it was time to start cutting up big pieces of plastic with the razor saw. Fortunately the Manchester required less surgery than the Lincoln, but

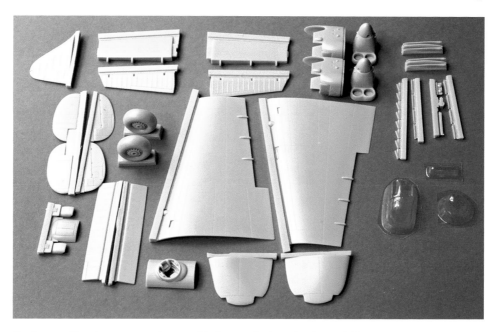

The Paragon Manchester conversion set with the parts laid out. (*Neil Woodall*)

The finished model from the port side. (*Neil Woodall*)

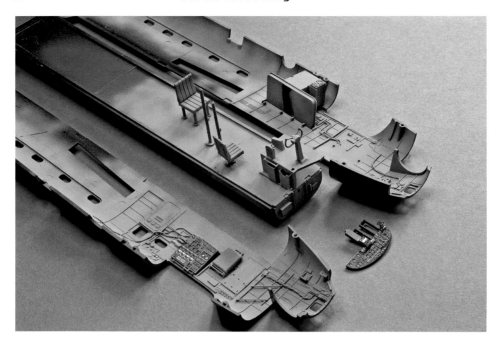

The fuselage interior painted up. (*Neil Woodall*)

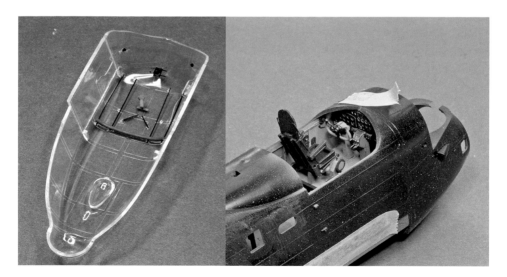

The cockpit canopy and the cockpit, now in the glued-together fuselage. (*Neil Woodall*)

care was still needed to get the cuts right. The outer Lancaster wings required removal on the dihedral kink line outboard of the inner engines, and the new outer wings needed grafting on. In principle, this is straightforward, but ensuring that the profile of the resin replacements accurately match the Tamiya wing and are substantial enough to survive handling requires some interior strengthening. The wing halves were removed from their tabs and glued together. Because the tabs were located along the leading edge, the result was somewhat untidy due to my clumsy approach, so some corrective work was going to be needed later on. Internal spars were added to the outer wings to increase strength and prevent compression when handling the model, and new spars were constructed from Evergreen plasticard to bridge the new join. This meant getting the dihedral kink angle correct as well as putting an angle in to accommodate the tapering of the Manchester's outer wings. The kink angle was copied from a forward view drawing on paper then transferred to plastic. The taper angle was simply achieved by bending the plastic to shape and test fitting the outer wings. After lots of dry fitting and removing slivers of plastic here and there on the spars, I eventually achieved the result I was looking for.

Because of the mess I'd made removing the tabs for the wings, I decided to make completely new leading edges from plasticard for the areas inboard of the intake scoop, rather than using filler. They were filed to a more consistent profile to allow the new leading edge to be grafted on, and then the whole profile was filed to restore the shape. The new intake scoops were made from plastic tube, and fortunately I had some clear tube of a suitable diameter for this task. The wing was drilled to allow the tube to feed in, the imperfections were filled, and the scoop was sanded to shape. The outer wings were then glued on to the inner wings using superglue, and double-checked for consistent dihedral across both wings.

The engines were next. The nacelles come in two halves, front and rear; however, when I removed them from their stubs, the front sections were slightly smaller in diameter than the rear parts, which confused me somewhat. There were two options: either simply glue them together and use filler to bridge the step; or insert a 2-mm spacer and fill the gap to allow a more natural profile. The latter option was taken because it meant less remedial work. The Paragon intake scoops above the nacelles looked slightly short when compared to reference photos, but this could have been because I had elongated the engines. I decided to fit them and used Milliput to extend the training edges back further to where they should have been. The engines grafted on to the wings beautifully. The resin outer wings had engraved panel lines, whereas the Tamiya inner wings had raised detail. To match things up, I extended the raised spar section using strips of 0.005-inch plasticard and engraved the other panel lines on the inboard sections to match the resin parts. Overall, this gave a consistency right across the span of the wing. The raised sections are somewhat overscale, most notably the spar line. I think this is due to a sealing tape that Tamiya has tried to represent having seen work being carried out on the BBMF Lancaster, but I chose to follow artistic licence over scale accuracy.

Returning to the fuselage, it was time to make the necessary corrections to turn it into a Manchester Mk I. Fortunately, the changes were limited. When I started the build, the intention was to build a variant with a mid-upper turret installed, so the part provided in the Paragon set needed to be installed. This required a section of the fuselage to be cut out.

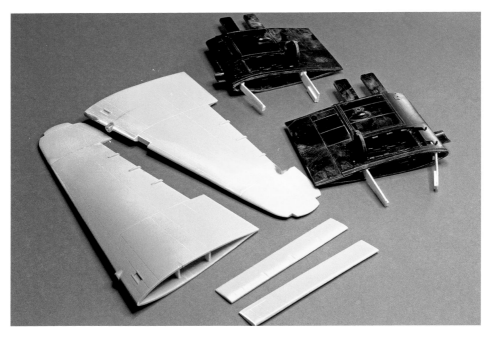

The wings with the Tamiya inner wings and the conversion set's outer wings. (*Neil Woodall*)

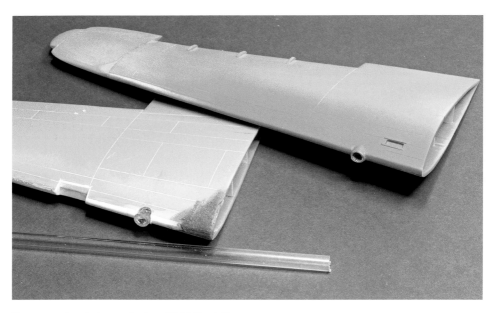

The outer wings being worked on. (*Neil Woodall*)

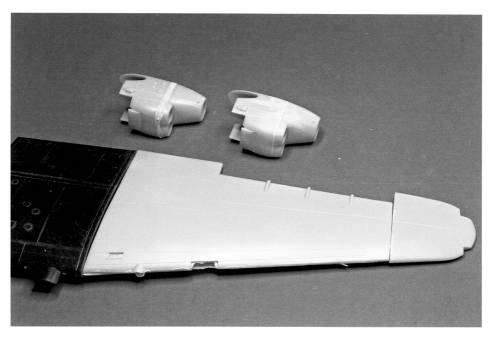

The port wing and Vulture nacelles being worked on. (*Neil Woodall*)

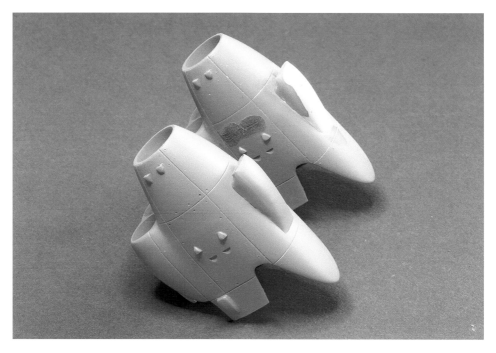

The nacelles primed, with a little more putty work being done on one. (*Neil Woodall*)

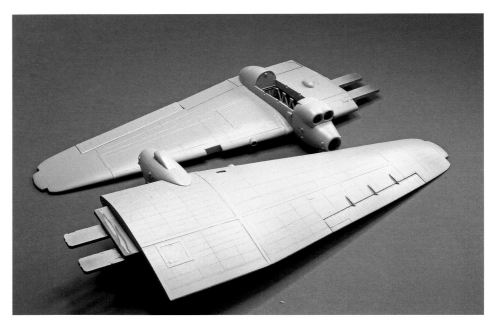

The completed wings, now primed. (*Neil Woodall*)

The measurements were made and masking tape was applied to mark the cut lines. My approach was to make the cuts slightly smaller than the part required, and to use files to open the gap up until it dropped into place. Later on, it was decided to model the aircraft as L7301, the aircraft in which Leslie Manser won his posthumous VC (Victoria Cross, the highest British military honour) on a tragic mission to Cologne. This aircraft never had a mid-upper turret, so the fairing was sanded off and the hole filled.

Because the aircraft being modelled was a Mk I and not a Mk Ia, it used the three-tail arrangement incorporating two smaller fins rather than the larger ones found on the Lancaster. All necessary parts were provided in the Paragon set. Only the first twenty-one Manchesters produced used the smaller span tail planes provided in the conversion set, so the Tamiya tail planes were used instead. Lancasters had metal-covered elevators introduced early on in production, but Manchesters had fabric ones. To replicate this effect, Tamiya masking tape was used to leave thin strips exposed on the elevators. Primer was sprayed on in several coats to build up a thickness and the masking was removed once dry. A light sanding with a sponge sanding stick took the hard edges off and another couple of coats of primer was applied to smooth the surfaces out, giving the fabric look. The other subtle difference on the small fins was a different style of rudder horn with a curved section that protruded through the tail forwards of the rudder. These were scratchbuilt using wire. The central tail fin was another fabric-covered surface. During manoeuvres it sometimes lost the fabric due to airflow issues over the mid-upper turret when installed. This part was secured in place by drilling a couple of holes in both the fuselage and mating surface of the fin, and inserting pieces of brass tube to act as locating pins.

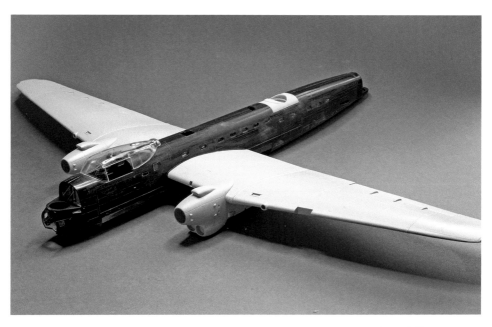

The completed wings joined to the fuselage. The tail still needs to be attached. (*Neil Woodall*)

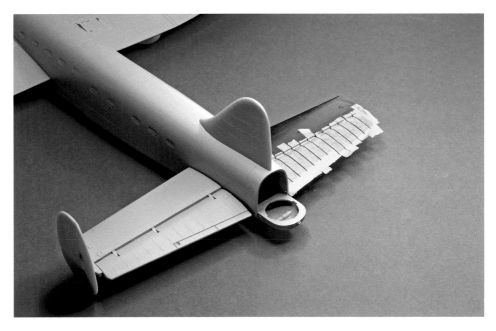

The tail parts added, with the lines for the fabric-covered elevators masked off for the starboard elevator, the port elevator already being finished. (*Neil Woodall*)

The other noticeable difference on Manchester Mk Is was the aerial mast protruding out of the rear of the cockpit. A slot was carefully cut using several small drill holes and the mast was cut from a piece of plasticard of a suitable thickness (1 mm approx.). The leading and trailing edges were rounded off. The mast was to be fitted at the end of the build so liquid mask was inserted into the slot to prevent paint from getting inside later on. Manchesters generally carried a much smaller bombload than Lancasters for obvious reasons relating to the powerplants and lifting capability. Unfortunately, the bomb bay floor in the Tamiya kit has huge locating pins for a full bomb load. Because of this, I needed to remove some of the pins, but it left the floor looking very untidy, and I wanted to have the bomb bay open. To get around this problem, I left the pins in place towards the centre section of the bomb bay and removed not only the pins, but also the floor structure detail in the front and aft areas. A new structure was fabricated from plasticard to at least make it presentable.

When the long row of fuselage windows was fitted, they were somewhat recessed in the openings when viewed from the outside rather than sitting flush. I decided to leave them in until the end of the build to act as masks, but after painting I would push them through and remove the excess plastic through the rear turret aperture. New windows would then be made from liquid Micro Kristal Klear.

The main parts of the kit were now complete. Before attaching the wings, the raised panel lines on the fuselage were sanded off and rescribed using the Olfa P-cutter 450 tool, giving a recessed finish. The whole aircraft was riveted using the RB productions riveting wheel, using approximate locations of rivet lines rather than a scientific application.

The aircraft was put to one side and work moved to the turrets. Fortunately, the need for a mid-upper turret was cancelled (the turret later went to good use on a Sanger Stirling Mk I), which meant that a little less work was required to finish the Manchester. The front FN5 turret on the Manchester was the same as the Lancaster, so this required no modification. Some additional internal framework was added to improve the look, however, and there is a slight error on the external side vertical framing of the Tamiya transparency. This was later remedied by lightly sanding the transparency to remove the marks and then correctly masking them at the time of painting. The front turret has ammunition boxes attached and if you follow the instructions, you should fit them prior to the fuselage assembly. To get around this, I glued the ammunition boxes to the fuselage to allow me to insert the turret at the end. The rear turret was different to the later FN20 used on the Lancaster. The correct FN4 was provided in the Paragon set with a vacuformed transparency and resin rear section with doors moulded in. I used the base and internal framework of the FN20 turret provided by Tamiya, but then built up the detail to mate it neatly to the replacement cupola. The framework on the cupola was made of thin strips of Solartrim, which has a self-adhesive backing and can be purchased cheaply. My normal approach is to dip the transparency in Johnson Klear, let it dry, and then add the Solartrim frames. Another dip in Klear helped to prevent the frames from peeling away afterwards. The gun barrels were replaced by Quickboost resin parts, which are far better detailed and relatively cheap. To attach them, the old barrels were removed and holes were drilled into the base to fit the resin barrels.

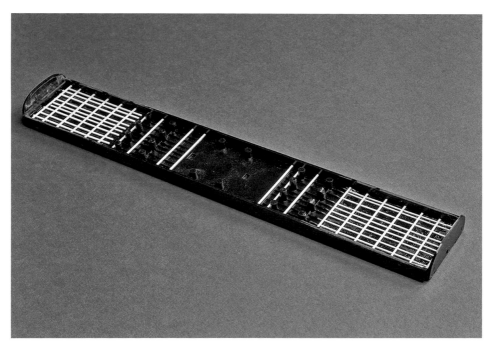

The bomb bay with extra parts being added to it. The added parts are in white polystyrene. (*Neil Woodall*)

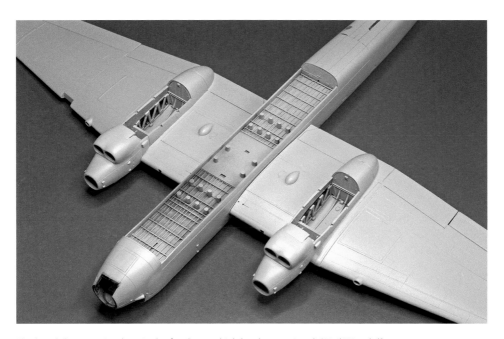

The bomb bay now in place in the fuselage, which has been primed. (*Neil Woodall*)

The primed fuselage and wings from the port side. The radio antenna has now been added through the back of the cockpit canopy. (*Neil Woodall*)

The turrets being worked on. Solartrim strips have been used for the framework. (*Neil Woodall*)

The clear parts on the build were masked using the Eduard masking set for the Lancaster. Because of the corrections on the front turret, I had to cut these parts manually, but that was straightforward. The standard Bomber Command colours of dark earth/dark green and overnight black were reproduced using Tamiya XF-81 Dark Green 2, Mr Hobby H072 Dark Earth, and Tamiya XF-85 Rubber Black. I used my trusty airbrush Hansa 381 with the 0.3-mm needle, which caters for most needs.

To try to emulate the rippling in the panels, a slightly lightened shade was mixed for each colour after the base colour was down, and a strip of masking tape was applied to a panel or rivet line. Here I airbrushed against the tape with the flow turned right down so that there was a subtle variation that looked like changes in light reflection. Doing this for both vertical and horizontal panel lines was very time-consuming and unfortunately difficult to show in the photographs, but it is more noticeable in real life.

This particular aircraft had a wavy demarcation line. I've found the easiest way to approach this is to roll a long sausage of Blu Tack and apply it to the area of the line. Using a brush or modelling tool handle, I simply push the handle in to the Blu Tack to get the desired look. Between each colour application, a coat of Johnson Klear was applied to help protect the paint from possible lifting when removing masking tape, and to provide a gloss base for the decals to prevent silvering.

There was no nose art on this aircraft so generic decals were used to cater for the roundels and codes. Xtradecal X48032 sheet was used to provide the Type A1 fuselage roundels. Looking at various photos of Manchesters, they appeared to use a variety of diameter roundels on the fuselage so it's worth doing some research beforehand. The

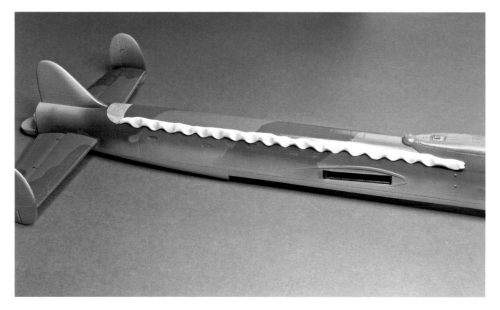

Blu Tack was applied to the fuselage as a mask for the wavy dividing line on the fuselage between the topside colours and the underside black. (*Neil Woodall*)

48-inch medium sea grey squadron codes came from the Xtradecal X48-050 sheet, while the small 8-inch grey codes came from the Ventura Decals V4853 sheet. Unlike the Lancaster, which had red stencilling on the undersides, early Manchesters had grey markings, so I opted to paint the most prominent ones by masking the areas first and spraying them on. The upper wing decals were taken from the Tamiya decal sheet.

Once the decals were on, the whole aircraft was given a coat of Klear to seal them in. A weathering wash was then applied to bring out the panel lines and rivet detail. Mig 1618 Deep Brown was applied over the upper surfaces, left for a few minutes, and then wiped off in the direction of the airflow. I do not like to leave it too long although some do allow it almost to dry. I prefer to have a very subtle panel line rather than a heavy one, unless photos show it to be required.

The black surfaces got a similar treatment using Mig 1615 Stone Grey. Once dry, the model was sprayed with a light coating of Alclad matt varnish. The weathering was built up further using soft pastels on a stubby small brush worked into the panel lines, with more around the engines and inner wing walkways. Looking at photos, exhaust stains were typically prominent on the Manchester, and with four exhaust banks per engine they made for an interesting effect. Initially, I applied very thin passes of highly thinned Tamiya rubber black mixed with XF-64 red brown, and then went over the top with XF-57 Buff to simulate the light areas caused by lean mixture running. A small amount of paint chipping was done with a silver pencil, typically leading-edge areas and walkways suffered this effect most noticeably. Some Manchesters were heavily weathered and worn-looking in photographic references, but I kept things quite reserved on this build, just enough to add interest.

Once the weathering was complete, a further coat of Alclad matt varnish was applied to give the desired finish and seal the pastels in. Rather than simply applying an even coat of varnish, I tend to apply more to panel lines as this gives a varied sheen across the surface. This is something that can be observed on real aircraft and also adds some further interest to the overall finish of the build. Unfortunately, it does not show up that well in photographs.

The final step was to remove the masks from the clear parts and glue the turrets in place and fit the propellers. This is where the last hurdle lay. The blades in the set were too small in diameter, and more suitable to a 1/72 scale Manchester. The easiest solution was to use a 1/32 scale Spitfire Mk I propeller as the profile was very similar, the diameter almost spot on, and aftermarket ones were readily available. The only drawback is that the Merlin turned the opposite way to the Vulture, but I felt that this was the best compromise to make, although some would disagree.

A detail that has not been covered in the build is the type of bomb bay door used on the real aircraft. The Manchester design started out using doors with a flat profile, looking side on to the aircraft, but the bomb bay could not accommodate the 4,000-lb Cookie without the doors being left partially open. I believe the doors were gradually replaced with the standard design fitted to the Lancaster, but given the constant modifications in the field, it's difficult to know whether this aircraft would have had the newer doors fitted or not. Given that neither the Paragon kit nor any other Manchester conversion kit includes flat doors, I chose to simply use the Tamiya Lancaster doors.

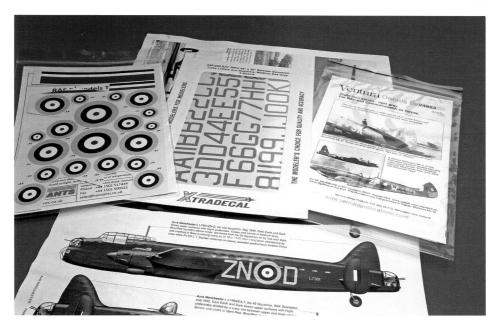

The decals (transfers) to be used on the model. (*Neil Woodall*)

The model in its jig, having some final work done. (*Neil Woodall*)

A close-up of the front of the fuselage. (*Neil Woodall*)

A photograph of the top. Note the red rectangle on the inner starboard wing for the stowed dinghy. (*Neil Woodall*)

The completed model from the starboard side. (*Neil Woodall*)

The tail surfaces of the finished model. (*Neil Woodall*)

Overall, the build was very enjoyable and relatively straightforward for anyone used to doing resin conversions. I had been after one of these sets for years, so I was incredibly happy finally to have a completed 1/48 scale Manchester in my collection.

1/48 SCALE AVRO LINCOLN (FROM TAMIYA AVRO LANCASTER)

The RAF decided it would not be necessary to develop an entirely new aircraft to replace the Lancaster, but that a development of the Lancaster itself would be sufficient. Indeed, the Lincoln started out as the 'Lancaster IV', but in the end the changes, including a longer fuselage and longer wings, were extensive enough for the aircraft to be renamed the 'Lincoln'. Although arriving too late for use in the Second World War, the Lincoln served with the RAF as a bomber into the second half of the 1950s, and was not retired from RAF service until 1963, having seen action in Aden, Kenya, and Malaya. It also saw service with Argentina and Australia (and saw service trials with Canada). In Argentine service it was in use until 1967. As with the previous Manchester conversion, the 1/48 scale Tamiya Lancaster kit serves as the basis (or donor kit) for this conversion, although the end result is quite a different aeroplane from the Manchester.

1/48 Scale Avro Lincoln Paragon Resin Conversion Set by Neil Woodall

The Avro Lincoln never gained the fame of its mother, the Lancaster. Born out of a development planned to support the war in the Pacific, the war ended before it got the chance to prove its worth. Aviation was also entering a period of significant change with the advent of the jet engine, which precipitated rapid development of aircraft design. Despite arguments about its obsolescence, the Lincoln did successfully support military action in Kenya and the Malayan Emergency in the 1950s.

There are currently few options for producing a 1/48 scale Bomber Command heavy of any type, so when I had the opportunity of purchasing a rare Paragon Lincoln resin conversion for a reasonable price, I snapped it up. This beautifully produced set is designed for the venerable Tamiya Lancaster which, despite its age, holds up well in the twenty-first century under a good coat of paint. As with all Lincoln conversions, it essentially requires the Lancaster fuselage to be cut up and an extension plug inserted just aft of the bomb bay, and for a new nose to be grafted on. The engine replacements are the other key change, but there are also lots of smaller changes that I'll mention along the way.

Although I sourced the conversion set for a relatively reasonable price, it was still an expensive build as the Tamiya Lancaster holds its price well. I was somewhat nervous at the idea of starting the build by chopping everything up, but it had to be done.

The conversion started with the wings. This was relatively straightforward as it simply required the wing tips to be cut off using a razor saw and the resin extensions grafted on. The risk here was that the join would be weak. To ensure the new tips would not break off, spars were made from Evergreen plasticard. These also served to strengthen the existing wing in the absence of the kit tips. The fit of the new tips was very good, but inevitably there was some blending to be done using Squadron green filler.

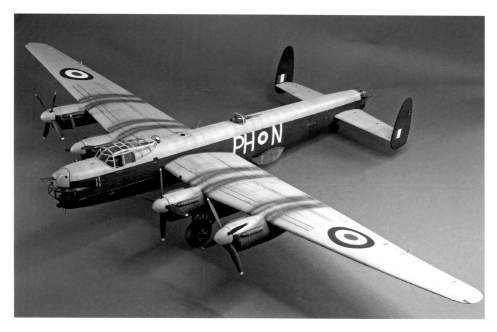

The completed model from the port side. (*Neil Woodall*)

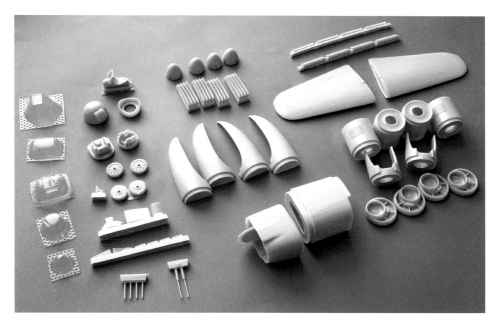

The Paragon Lincoln conversion set with the parts laid out. (*Neil Woodall*)

The detail on the Tamiya wing surfaces is predominantly raised, so while some recessed lines were added right across the span using an Olfa P-Cutter 450 scribing tool, I chose to replace the Tamiya raised wing tip join with a new raised strip using plasticard. This was presumably intended to replicate a sealing tape.

The next task was to cut up the fuselage so that the extension plug and new nose could be added later. The cut lines were marked with Tamiya masking tape and, again, the razor saw was used to carefully cut up the fuselage halves. At this point, focus turned to the interior, so the fuselage halves were put aside for the time being.

The interior was largely completed using the standard Tamiya parts, although the Eduard pre-painted photoetched parts were added and some minor scratchbuilding was done to improve the areas visible through the large canopy. The pilot's seat is quite sparse in detail so additional framework to replicate the hinged head armour and lower structure was added. Not captured in the photos, the canopy interior was also detailed, including upper curtains, curtain rails, and a few odd details applied using PVA glue (often called 'white' glue) so as not to leave glue marks on the clear areas. As the interior is black on the Lincoln, I simply used Vallejo black primer then varied the panels slightly by adding a drop of Tamiya white into it. The windows were also glued into place during the internal assembly stage. The Lincoln did not have the long row of fuselage windows that the early Lancasters had, so the intent at this stage was to fit them and later to fill them flush and over paint them.

Returning to the fuselage assembly, an important note on the Lincoln is that you do not simply insert a plug and make the Lancaster fuselage longer. The rear end was canted upwards by 1.5 degrees to reduce the angle of attack on the tail plane, I believe, and the conversions I've completed to date do not mention this requirement. This was addressed by cutting another section out of the rear fuselage and adding spacers into the lower surface and internal strips of plastic to secure everything together. There was no detailed measurement here; I simply did it by eyeball using a steel rule to determine if the upper spine looked about right when compared to available drawings. I experienced a slight setback on this build in that the extension plug appeared to suffer shrinkage on the forward end, meaning that I had to reverse it for a better fit. This meant removing part of the full circumference tab designed to act as a sleeve for the rear fuselage as it now fouled the bomb bay. In hindsight, potentially I could have left the tab in place as I chose to have the bomb bay doors closed later on.

Despite the extension plug being generally a good fit, there was further work required to ensure that the long fuselage looked straight and not stepped or wonky. To address this, P38 two-part car filler was used. This is my preferred filler for large surfaces because most modelling fillers I've used suffer shrinkage in the months following a build. In addition to its lack of shrinkage, P38 dries very quickly and is easy to sand. Several cycles of fill, sand and prime followed until I was happy with the finish.

I used Tamiya light grey primer from the aerosol can throughout the build. It allows you to see imperfections in the surface and can also assist in filling minor blemishes once given a light sanding. The mid-upper turret on the Lincoln is positioned further forwards than that of the Lancaster Mk I/III, but is much the same as the later Mk VII, so the existing hole was filled with the plug provided in the Tamiya kit and a new hole was drilled

The wingtip sawed off in preparation for the attachment of the Lincoln wing extensions. (*Neil Woodall*)

The wing tip being worked on. (*Neil Woodall*)

The cockpit interior being worked on. (*Neil Woodall*)

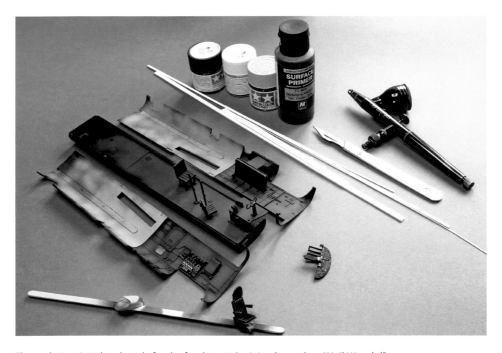

The cockpit painted and ready for the fuselage to be joined together. (*Neil Woodall*)

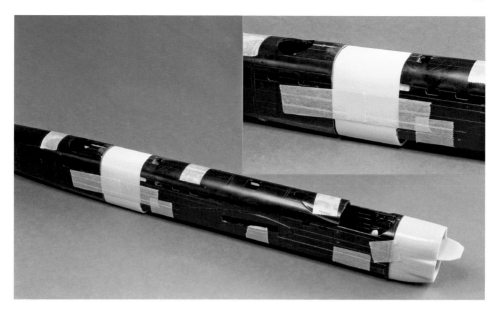

The fuselage glued together with the resin fuselage plug and resin nose attached. (*Neil Woodall*)

Spacers or shims need to be added to the aft fuselage to acheive the correct angle. (*Neil Woodall*)

further forwards where the rear hatch normally resides. A new recessed turret housing is provided in the Paragon set to help with this step. Again, everything was blended in using P38 filler. The slightly protruding beam above the bomb bay on each side of the fuselage was extended using more plasticard (0.005-inch) and the join to the original profile was blended in with Squadron filler.

Another subtle change on later Lancasters and the Lincoln was a more protruding rear turret airflow deflector at the end of the rear fuselage. This was scratchbuilt using more Evergreen plasticard filed down on one edge and again blended in. With the interior now fitted, the fuselage could be joined up and the resin nose added. The fit was excellent but something did not quite look right, and it took me a while to figure it out. The chin below the bomb aimer panel was too raked, so P38 filler was used again to correct the profile. The detail moulded onto the part was carefully cut off using the trusty razor saw and then added back on to the reprofiled chin afterwards. A small amount of filler was used to fully blend the nose join into the main fuselage.

Attention now moved back to the wings. While still using Merlin engines, the profile of the nacelle was quite different to the Lancaster due to the annular radiators. As such, new engines are provided in the Paragon set along with four-blade propellers and hubs. Attaching the new engines was relatively straightforward, with the only cutting required being to the main gear fairings under the inner wings. These needed to be reattached to the Paragon forward nacelles, and a small amount of filler did the trick.

With the wings assembled, the lump of resin and plastic was beginning to look like a Lincoln. At this point, the whole model was 'riveted' using an RB Productions riveting wheel on a Swann Morton handle. This is somewhat time-consuming but along

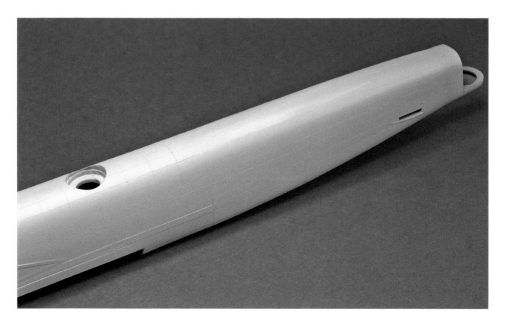

The aft fuselage after shimming, filling, sanding, and priming. (*Neil Woodall*)

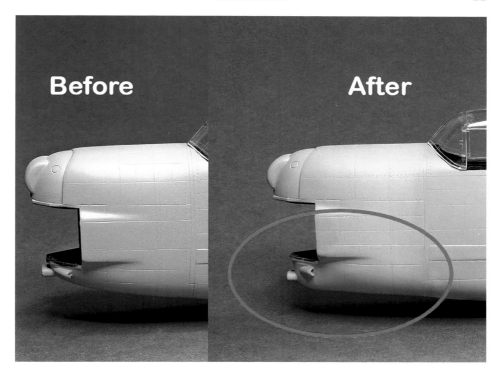

The bottom of the nose is too shallow so it has to be built up deeper, as shown here. (*Neil Woodall*)

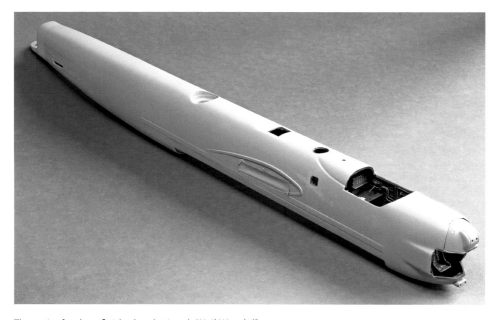

The entire fuselage finished and primed. (*Neil Woodall*)

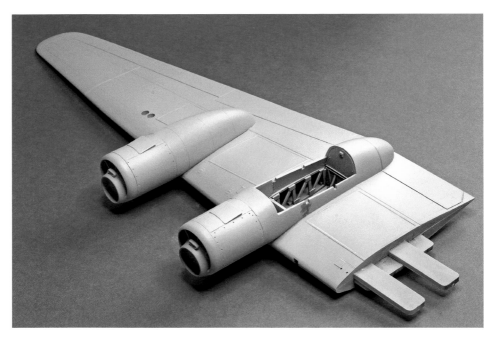

The port wing, with a little filling and sanding still to be done on the inboard nacelle. (*Neil Woodall*)

The nearly completed model, missing its vertical tail planes. (*Neil Woodall*)

with the rescribed panel lines, the overall look of the build is enhanced. Some of the transparencies on the Lincoln are different to those on the Lancaster, most notably the angular bomb aimer panel. On the real aircraft this new nose design not only eliminated distortion from the curved plexiglass dome, but I read somewhere that it also improved maximum speed by around 5 mph. Also included in the kit is the taller astrodome and the correct turrets for the Lincoln made from vacuformed transparencies. These are the Bristol B.17 turret with two huge 20-mm cannons and a Boulton Paul Type D turret with two 0.50 Browning guns. This replaced the tried and tested Frazer Nash FN20 on the Lancaster, which was equipped with four of the smaller 0.303-calibre guns. Handling vacuformed clear parts can be difficult if you're not used to them due to their thinness and flexibility, but once dipped in Johnson Klear, they produce beautiful distortion-free replicas. I tend to carefully squash a ball of Blu Tack inside vacuform turrets to give some rigidity, which helps when cutting them away from the sheet using a new Swann Morton modelling blade. Afterwards, a gentle wash in dishwashing liquid removes any residue left by the Blu Tack.

Another subtle difference between the Lancaster and Lincoln are the tail fins under the rudder yaw tabs. The Paragon kit provides replacement parts necessitating the Tamiya section of the same size to be cut away allowing the replacement to drop in. The replacement parts mean that the cuts are done on panel lines reducing the risk of the cut line being visible afterwards.

With the bulk of the assembly work done, it was soon time to move on to painting. Before it could commence, however, the H2S radome needed fitting and the clear parts required masking. Unfortunately, the huge clear H2S radome did not come with the conversion set, but I managed to source one separately from the same place. Normally, I try to get clear parts as clear and shiny as possible, but this large ungainly unit hung underneath where it would have been subjected to all sorts of debris and grime from ground handling. As such, it was given a light airbrush of Alclad matt varnish. The overlapping frames were created by masking them and applying matt varnish with a drop of Tamiya white paint mixed in.

For the masking of the clear parts, I took the easy route with the cockpit and used the superb, if somewhat expensive, Eduard canopy mask set. The bomb aimer's panel, however, had to be done the old-fashioned way, so Tamiya tape was applied one panel at a time and burnished in using a cocktail stick before the excess was trimmed off using a small, curved Swann Morton blade. The two-tone colour scheme of medium sea grey over night black was achieved by using acrylic Tamiya XF-85 Rubber Black and XF-83 Medium Sea Grey 2. Each of the colours was applied out of the jar, then a drop of Tamiya white was added and applied to each panel to replicate a slight weathering. Diluted with X-20 thinner at a ratio of approximately 1/1, the colours were applied using a Hansa 381 airbrush fitted with a 0.3-mm needle. The grey was sprayed first, and then, for two reasons, a coat of Johnson Klear was sprayed over the top: First, to provide a gloss finish to reduce silvering when the decals were being added; secondly, to reduce the risk of paint lifting under the masking tape, which has happened previously. Once dry, the demarcation line was carefully applied using 10-mm Tamiya masking tape, and the upper surfaces were masked by a combination of Tamiya tape and kitchen roll. Because of the long fuselage, it would have been easy to

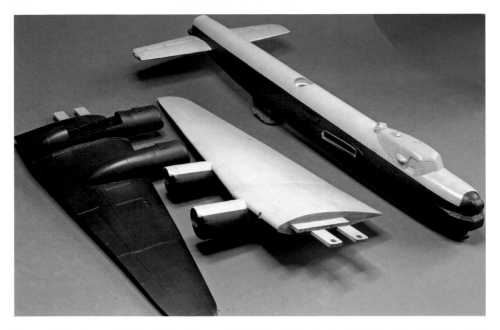

The model has been painted, with the wings painted before being attached to the fuselage. (*Neil Woodall*)

end up with a curved or wavy demarcation line, so I double-checked and triple-checked for straightness before committing to the position (learning from past experience!). Once the Rubber Black was applied, this too got a coat of Klear over the top after removing the masking tape protecting the grey areas.

The decals were comprised from generic decal sheets. The roundels came from the Xtradecal set X037-48 (Type D Roundels and fin flashes), the white 48-inch squadron codes were from the Colorado 48.53 set, and the red 8-inch serial codes were from Xtradecal sheet X48049. Because I was building an aircraft with a mid-upper turret and wanted Type D roundels, the choice of schemes was quite limited as many later aircraft had the turrets removed. In the end, I chose RA679 of 12 Squadron, which eventually came to grief after an overshoot on three engines when landing at RAF Binbrook.

After application and the removal of excess water, I applied Daco Products Medium Decal Set to the decals to help bed them down. Initially, this causes the decal to ripple which is quite alarming on first use, but it soon dries and performs its magic! The Lincoln had various stencils, many of which were coloured yellow on the vast black fuselage areas, but I did not have many to hand. I managed to cobble together a few from the spares pile, but unfortunately had to leave it looking somewhat sparse compared to the reference photos I used in the build. Fortunately, the wing decals from the Lancaster set met most of the needs for the Lincoln, in particular the wing walkway lines and 'no step' lettering. Once the decals were on, a final coat of Johnson Klear was sprayed on to seal the decals in before weathering.

Weathering began on the grey upper surfaces using Mig Deep Brown (A.Mig-1619). It was washed over and left for a few minutes before wiping over with a kitchen towel in

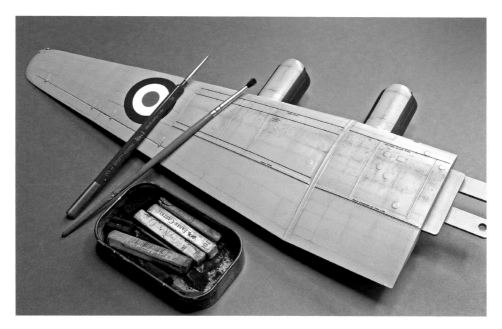

Weathering on the port wing, done with brushes and pastels. (*Neil Woodall*)

the direction of airflow to pick out the panel lines. For the large expanse of black, a Mig Stone Grey (A.Mig-1615) was applied in the same way. It was at this point that all the effort spent in rescribing became visibly worthwhile.

There are various ways to weather an aircraft model, some people pre-shade, some post-shade, and some use oil paints, but those are things I have not mastered yet. My preferred approach is to pick out panel lines using soft pastel. To apply the pastels, first the surface needs a matt finish to grip to, so a light coating of Alclad Matt Varnish was applied. I try to use photos of real aircraft to replicate weathering rather than applying a one-size-fits-all across the entire aircraft. Typically, areas around the engines and high traffic walkways on the wings get the dirtiest. With this in mind, a small stubby brush was used to work brown and black soft pastel into the panel lines with heavier areas around the engines. Again, using a kitchen towel or larger brush, excess pastel was lightly brushed away in the direction of the airflow.

Towards the end of the build, the wheels, exhausts and various aerials were added. I had some issues getting a tight fit of the exhaust stacks against the rounded engine surfaces, so I carefully scraped the centre away using a small, curved blade so that the facing surface more closely matched the rounded engine profile. Notable on the Lincoln and Lancaster was exhaust staining on the upper and lower wings. At high power settings, the staining was black, but on leaned out mixtures, the staining (caused by lead content, I believe) was much lighter. To recreate this effect, I first applied an XF-85 Rubber Black/XF-64 Red Brown mixture using the airbrush. This was a very diluted mixture applied in lots of passes with the flow turned right down on the airbrush to prevent any

Exhaust stains have been applied to the wings. (*Neil Woodall*)

noticeable mistakes. Afterwards, the centre areas were sprayed with Tamiya XF-57 Buff to represent the leaned mixture stains in the same way. A further effort with the stubby brush and soft pastels was carried out to blend the exhaust staining into the panel line dirt. Then the whole aircraft was sealed with a further coat of Alclad matt varnish.

With the painting, decalling and weathering complete, the next step was that most nerve-wracking one: the removing of the masking from the clear parts. There is always the risk of paint bleeds, glue marks or dust build up on the inside caused by static. Being acrylic paint, where bleeding does occur, it can usually be cleaned up using a cocktail stick. Fortunately, on this build there was little to clean up. If dust does get in there, finding a hole somewhere and using either a keyboard aerosol cleaner or a rubber squeezy bulb can do the trick.

The final part of the build was the assembly of the rear and mid-upper turrets. The rear was somewhat fiddly due to the thin vacuform parts, so a great deal of care (and inappropriate language!) was taken to ensure that the rear of the turret aligned well with the glazing. The long 20-mm cannon barrels for the mid-upper turret are provided in resin, but are quite flexible and tend to bend. On a previous 1/72 scale conversion, I replicated the barrels using Albion Alloys brass tube, and at some point I may do the same for this build to eliminate the bending problem.

The finished aircraft is considerably heavier than an equivalent Lancaster build due to the resin content; however, the Tamiya landing gear is up to the job of supporting it. The two VHF aerials on the spine between the canopy and mid-upper turret were made from stretched sprue. Small holes were drilled into the fuselage to allow them to be glued in to place and take a knock without coming off.

A close-up of the fuselage of the completed model. (*Neil Woodall*)

The completed model from the starboard side. (*Neil Woodall*)

The completed model from the front. (*Neil Woodall*)

2
Resin/Vacuform Models

Resin and vacuform kits have long filled a void left by mainstream model companies, who tend to go for more well-known (and well-selling) subjects, such as the ubiquitous Bf 109 and P-51 Mustang. For a long time, only resin or vacuform kits have been available for some aircraft. This section will cover how to build these kits, which although not necessarily more complicated or difficult to build than their injection-moulded counterparts, do require some different techniques and skills.

Vacuform kits are created by having a heat-softened sheet of polystyrene plastic draped over either a raised form (male) or sucked into a cavity mould (female) using a vacuum, hence the term 'vacuform' (or 'vacform', or 'vacuum-formed'). The female moulding allows for more detail to be formed into the vacuformed sheet. Some vacuform kits are very basic, offering nothing more than the essential parts of the aeroplane such as the fuselage, wings, and tail planes. In these cases you must provide everything else yourself, including landing gear, interior, propellers, etc. Decals are often absent. However, for some aircraft, the only kits available are vacuform kits. I do not see a mainstream manufacturer coming out with an injection-moulded kit of the Blackburn Perth flying boat anytime soon, for example.

Resin kits substitute polyurethane resin for the polystyrene plastic used in injection-moulded and vacuform kits, with the resin being poured into rubberised moulds. At first these kits were rather simple and crude, but some manufacturers, such as Prop & Jet out of Russia, now create kits that are beautifully moulded and, in terms of detail, the equal of anything in injection-moulded plastic. There are unfortunately some disadvantages to resin: the resin dust created by sanding might be dangerous to your health (use a mask); the parts can sometimes be prone to warping or sagging (which can worsen with time); there are often bubbles present in the resin; superglue adhesives (cyanoacrylates) or epoxies must be used to attach the parts together; and the kits are often quite expensive. Nonetheless, resin kits offer many kits of aircraft that have never appeared as injection-moulded or even vacuform kits.

Large resin kits, where fibreglass resin is used for the main parts, and polystyrene for everything else, are now available from a few manufacturers in Eastern Europe such as

Amodel and Modelsvit. They cover huge subjects, such as post-war Soviet bombers and transports, in 1/72 scale. These kits differ from the traditional polyurethane resin kits in that the medium used, fibreglass resin, is very hard, whereas polyurethane resin is usually quite soft. This medium is more difficult to work with because of its hardness, but its rigidity makes it less prone to warping or sagging, which is important with the huge kits it is used for. The resin kit in this section is made of the more usual polyurethane resin variety.

1/72 SCALE SUPERMARINE SCIMITAR—RESIN

The Scimitar was a carrier-based twin-jet British interceptor of the 1950s and 1960s. It was the last aircraft of the famous Supermarine company to be produced, and is noteworthy for that alone. There are several injection-moulded plastic kits of the Scimitar in 1/72 scale, but the most accurate and detailed kit was made by Czech Master (CMR) in full resin, although this detail came at a premium. This kit can be made into an excellent and detailed representation of the Scimitar, as is shown by the build below.

1/72 Scale Czech Master Resin Supermarine Scimitar F.1 by Bill Gilman

I've been seduced by the dark side. The side that conventional styrene adhesives do not stick to. The side that can shock you more than the price of a litre of petrol. You know the side I speak of—resin modelling!

CMR's 1/72 scale Scimitar is a beautiful multimedia kit that builds into a superb replica of the original. (*Bill Gilman*)

In this chapter, I'll build the 1/72 scale CMR kit of the Supermarine Scimitar F.1, a subject that has received scant attention from the major plastic kit manufacturers. The CMR kit includes everything you need—resin, photoetch, eight different marking schemes, extensive payloads, vacuformed canopies, painting masks—everything except plastic! In addition to the basic kit, I'll also use the CMR folding wing set, which was a separate purchase. The instruction sheets run to eighteen pages, and there are many colour and black and white reference photos. What follows, then, is an out-of-the-box build, one that I hope will entice you to try out this side of our fascinating hobby.

WHY RESIN?

That's a great question. Resin can produce extremely crisp detail, and plenty of it. This is due to the flexibility of the mould and its ability to produce very sharp corners, small details, and thin surfaces. Traditional injection moulding processes use rigid tooling and compromises must be made affecting things like wall thickness, draft angles, and corner radii. To amortise this expensive tooling, large production runs must be made, limiting subjects to those likely to sell in large quantities.

Resin is an ideal way to produce those unusual subjects you've wanted to appear in kit form, often with a level of detail you do not see with injection moulding. The downsides are that it takes longer to produce a resin kit, the production runs are smaller, and the manufacturers are often cottage industries. This means that the cost of the kit is usually several times higher than a comparable injection kit. But if you're like me, you load up your injection kits with all sorts of aftermarket accessories anyway, and when you look at what is contained in the CMR kit of the Scimitar, there's no need for any aftermarket at all. The value then looks much more comparable.

Photoetched parts allow accurate to-scale depictions of details like the Scimitar's air brakes. (*Bill Gilman*)

FIRST THINGS FIRST

First, let's talk about safety. Whether it is razor saws, scribing tools, paints or adhesives, modelling comes with tools that must be handled with care and respect. Resin kits are no different, especially when it comes to the dust generated by sawing and sanding. Wet sanding can reduce the amount of airborne dust but always use a particle mask over your nose and mouth whenever you grind, sand, or saw. If you use an electric tool, a respirator mask is recommended.

Second, forget about liquid styrene adhesives; they will not work with resin. A good choice for resin parts is cyanoacrylate (superglue), unless it needs to be an especially strong bond in which case a 'five-minute' epoxy is a good choice. Small parts can be attached with specialty adhesives such as 'Gator's Grip'. I use this quite often to attach photoetched parts, too.

And thirdly, where are the sprues? Most resin kits are produced with low-pressure casting techniques like those used for resin aftermarket parts. Consequently, the parts are attached to blocks of resin called 'pour' or 'casting' blocks and must be carefully removed to avoid damage. A razor saw is ideal for removing the part from the pour block. Do not try to cut exactly at the edge of the part—leave some of the pour block attached and carefully remove it afterwards with a sanding stick. This helps avoid damage to the part from a slip of the saw. Also, it is common for several parts to be attached to the same pour block, and these are often the smallest parts. Extra care *always* pays off at this stage.

THE BUILD

The first thing to do is separate the parts from the pour blocks. I usually do this one subassembly at a time. When sanding or grinding resin, always remember that material will be removed much faster than with styrene. It's very easy to overdo it. Sand a little at a time, and test fit often.

When cleaning the fuselage halves, it's critical to get the mating surfaces flat and even. I've found one of the best ways to do this is to tape a large piece of sandpaper onto a flat surface—I use an old windowpane—and sand the fuselage in much the same way as you would a vacuform kit. By maintaining contact between the fuselage and the sandpaper, you'll end up with nice flat mating surfaces. Remember to sand a little at a time, alternating the two fuselage halves, and test fit often!

It's also important to check for any casting flaws such as pinholes. I found a few, and these were filled with an automotive spot glazing putty.

Painting work commenced with the cockpit and the other parts that go inside the fuselage. The cockpit on the real Scimitar was black, but in this scale, I like to use a dark grey, so details will be more visible. Otherwise, everything gets lost in a 'coal hole'. CMR include a pre-painted photoetched instrument panel, but for reasons unfathomable, it's a medium grey colour. Using a very fine detail brush, I hand painted over the medium grey to match the cockpit colour.

Although the cockpit grey looks light in the photo (especially with the photo lights), once the fuselage is closed up it looks much darker. Details were picked out on the consoles and on the sidewalls by brush, and the harnesses and pull handle on the ejection seat came from the pre-painted photoetched fret included with the kit. Rudder pedals were added as a final touch.

Carefully remove and clean up the parts that will go inside the fuselage—it's easy to overdo it. (*Bill Gilman*)

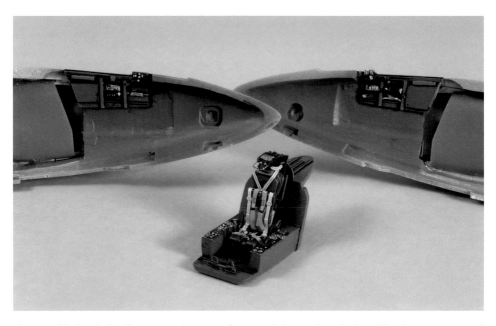

This superbly detailed cockpit is a combination of resin and photoetch, and a bit of detail painting too. (*Bill Gilman*)

The intakes, front gear bay, and the arresting hook bay were painted aluminium with a dark grey wash. After adding the cockpit to the starboard fuselage, nose weight was needed, otherwise the Scimitar would be a tail-setter. CMR do not say how much weight to add, so I taped all the major components together (wings, etc.) and tried different amounts. I think I overdid it, but that's better than not having enough!

The interior details were added, and the fuselage halves joined. This can be tricky with a resin kit, as they do not typically have locating pegs. I use superglue, but I do not run a bead all the way around and try to put the two halves together all at once. Glue a small area to start with, and then work your way around, gluing additional small areas one at a time. The alignment of the two halves is critical as you start the gluing process. Any error at the first step will be amplified as you go along. The starting point is chosen so that any potential fit problems are minimised, and hopefully any mismatches end up on the bottom. For this kit I chose the seam on the top spine because I wanted to make sure the panel lines aligned properly. As you work your way around, make sure the glue in each area cures completely before you move on to the next step. You'll see that the gap between the fuselage halves will get smaller and smaller as you move around. To place the superglue into the gap, I use a No. 11 blade, since it can slide in-between the fuselage halves easily.

There was not too much fettling needed to make everything fit together. Once both halves were joined, I ran a bead of superglue along the seam. This not only reinforces the bond, but it can be sanded smooth and scribes well, so you can reconnect the panel lines.

Now onto the wings. I removed the inner wings from the CMR folding wing set. There is amazing detail in the wing fold! But also, some problems: there is a very thin portion that protrudes past the wing fold on top of the wing. The one on the starboard wing was not completely formed and had cracked. I reinforced the crack with superglue and filled the crack with putty.

Since the wings are a butt join, it's a good idea to add reinforcing rods to strengthen the bond. I drilled holes and added short pieces of styrene tubing attached with epoxy. (I usually use brass tubing but was all out.) Corresponding holes to receive the tubing were drilled into the wings. Since it's quite difficult to have these sets of holes align perfectly, I made those in the wings slightly oversize, knowing that the epoxy would fill in any gaps.

The inner wings and the vertical tail were then added to the fuselage. Now she's starting to look like a Scimitar! There was a small amount of anhedral to the tailplanes, and I made good use of my references to get this set properly. The wing root area was puttied, primed, and sanded a few times until I was happy. This was the only part of the kit where the fit was a bit dodgy. A small amount of filler was used to blend the vertical tail into the fuselage spine, and the panel lines were rescribed across the fuselage seams and things looked ready for some paint.

I chose the markings for XD324, 158-R, aboard HMS *Ark Royal* in June of 1965, in the standard Extra Dark Sea Grey (EDSG) over White scheme. I began by painting the underside Gunze H11 Flat White but modulated in a random pattern with a slightly darker 'dirty' white. Small additional amounts of weathering were applied later in the build. The gear and arresting hook bays were masked off and painted aluminium with a dark grey wash.

Gluing the two fuselage halves together requires a different technique than that used for traditional kits. (*Bill Gilman*)

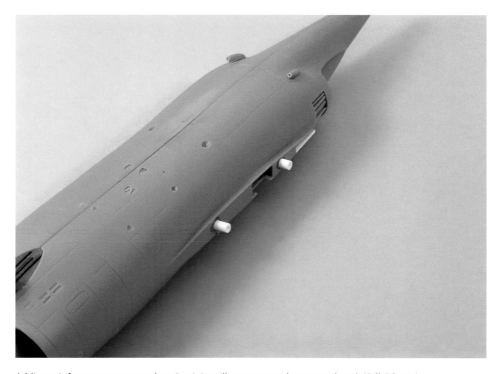

Adding reinforcement pegs to the wing join will create a much stronger bond. (*Bill Gilman*)

The wing roots required some filler, but the basic assembly is complete, and the model is taking shape. (*Bill Gilman*)

The underside white was post-shaded with an off-white to provide a basis for further weathering. (*Bill Gilman*)

Next was the EDSG. I masked everything carefully, including the sections that wrap around the leading edges of the wings and tailplanes. It's important to get the demarcation line in the right spot, so I spent quite some time studying on-line photos, profiles, drawings, and the CMR instructions. If you do not get this right, things look slightly askance. As it turns out, there are some panel lines which assisted in getting the demarcation line right. I used Gunze H333 EDSG, which was then post shaded with random patches of H331 Dark Sea Grey for effect.

The landing gear was painted aluminium, with chrome silver used for the oleo struts. CMR provide photoetched pieces for the brake lines and the oleo scissors, and the resin wheels were prepared with Gunze H77 Tire Black and a lighter grey post shading. The landing gear was added to the fuselage, and the Scimitar had legs!

At this point, I realised that I had forgotten to paint the inside of the intakes. This made for an intriguing masking job, especially since the EDSG and white paint wraps around the lip of each intake and into the intake trunk itself. A little perseverance with the tape, and all was well. Next time, though, I will paint this area before the fuselage goes together!

Next, the area inside the wing fold, the metal areas aft of the exhausts, and the interior of the air brake bays were painted. Several different shades of Alclad were used to match reference photographs. A light wash really brings out the detail in the wing fold and air brake bays—plus there are photoetched parts that provide additional detail.

The topside consists of random applications of Extra Dark Sea Grey and Dark Sea Grey. This prevents the model from looking monotone. (*Bill Gilman*)

A dark grey wash really brings out the detail in the resin castings. Note also the photoetched oleo scissors. (*Bill Gilman*)

The Scimitar has prominent boundary layer vanes inside each intake, and CMR provide for this with photoetched and resin parts. I'd waited until now to add these, as the EDSG and White paint goes underneath them. Since photoetched parts are nominally flat, folding is required to achieve the final orientation of the vanes. This was easily accomplished with long nose pliers (remember to use those without a serrated gripping surface to mar the parts). Try to make the fold only once, as repeated folding will result in the vane breaking off. Once the boundary layer assemblies are completed, they slide into the intake nicely, and really look the part.

Time for clear gloss varnish and the application of the decals. CMR provide decals for eight different schemes, along with a variety of stencils. Decal solvent was used to ensure the decals snuggled down over the surface details, and to minimise any silvering. I also painted and attached the gear doors at this time.

The air brakes are made from photoetched pieces, cleverly stacked upon each other to create a 3D sculptured piece. Although the air brakes were seldom deployed when the aircraft was on the ground, a little 'modeller's licence' allows us to add some nice detail to the model. Although these pieces are flat, the actual air brakes were curved slightly to follow the shape of the fuselage. Rolling the parts over a large wooden dowel adds the proper curve.

CMR provide two sets of vacuform canopies for the model, which is great news if you make a mistake cutting out the first one. Luckily, I managed to succeed on my first

Photoetched boundary layer vanes this thin could not be produced by injection moulding in 1/72 scale. (*Bill Gilman*)

The model now standing on its 'feet'. (*Bill Gilman*)

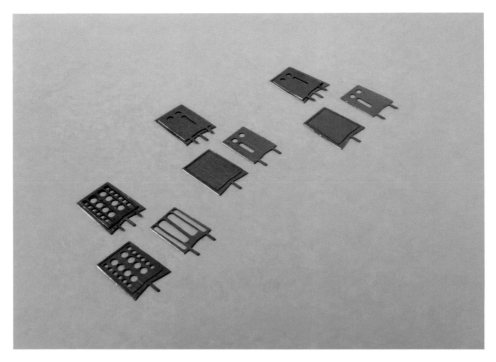

Each air brake (top row) is made from two photoetched components (bottom row). (*Bill Gilman*)

attempt, and the windscreen and sliding canopy were masked using the masks provided in the kit and prepared for paint. However, I found that I was unable to get a good fit between the bottom of the windscreen and the fuselage, most likely from my not cutting properly. This resulted in a slight gap that I filled with a small amount of Perfect Plastic Putty (PPP), since the fuselage was already painted and decaled. PPP can be 'sanded' and smoothed with water, and I used a wet paintbrush for the task. When I was satisfied that the windscreen blended into the fuselage nicely, I used the airbrush to carefully paint the blended area, making sure to protect the previously painted surfaces.

The outer wing sections were now painted to match the fuselage, and the markings applied. I then finished up the 150-gallon drop tanks, the airbrake petals, painted the canopy, and prepared the pylons and bombs.

I mounted the bombs on the respective pylons and added them to the outer wing sections. I suspect that you probably would not have live bombs on the plane when the wings were folded. But I think it looks good, and if I get taken to task for posing it this way, I can always claim it's a 'what if' model.

I then added the drop tanks, being careful to make sure that the pylon overlaps the wing fold area as it does on the real plane.

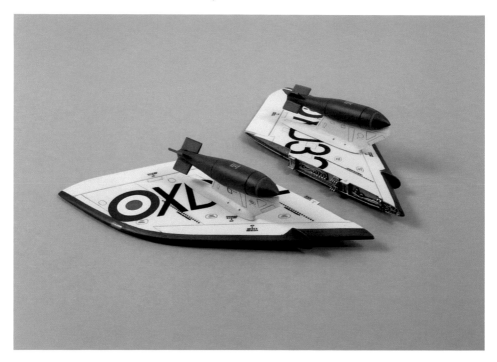

The finished folding wing segments are ready to be attached to the model. (*Bill Gilman*)

Finishing Up

CMR provide photoetched pieces for the wing braces (jury struts), but they are flat, and I substituted 0.6-mm diameter round styrene rod instead. All that's left to finish her up is to add the outer wings, additional photoetch in the wing fold area, add the struts and braces, the canopy, and a bunch of antennae.

Mounting the airbrakes in the open position was by far the fiddliest part of the build, especially getting them in the proper orientation and alignment. Luckily, I had some great photos to go by, and I'm happy with the result.

There we have it—a nicely detailed 1/72 scale Scimitar. As you can see, building a resin kit is not all that different to building an injection-moulded kit. The removal of resin parts from their casting blocks should present no problem for anyone who has used aftermarket resin parts, and once you get the hang of it, it's quite easy to do. Likewise, using superglue and epoxy is also quite straightforward. So, building a resin kit is not really difficult, it's just different. The time spent to learn new techniques is amply rewarded with exciting kits of unusual subjects, and highly detailed as well. After you've built your first few resin kits, you'll wonder what took you so long. Next thing you know, you'll be wanting to cast your own parts in resin, but that's the subject for another time. Happy modelling!

Attaching and aligning the six air brakes was the most fiddly part of the build. This really adds a lot to the attraction of the finished model. (*Bill Gilman*)

Round styrene rod was substituted for the kit's photoetched wing braces. (*Bill Gilman*)

The model does an excellent job of capturing the unique look and stance of Supermarine's last fighter for the Royal Navy. (*Bill Gilman*)

A worthy addition to any collection of FAA aircraft. (*Bill Gilman*)

One more parting shot of the exquisite CMR 1/72 scale Scimitar—a beautiful kit of a beautiful aircraft. (*Bill Gilman*)

1/32 SCALE HANDLEY PAGE HALIFAX GR.II

One area in which vacuform kits continue to be produced is in the form of very large kits, such as 1/32 scale bombers. This includes bombers such as the four-engined Handley Page Halifax, a strategic bomber of the Second World War, which is produced as a vacuform kit by Tigger Models. It is definitely not a kit for a beginner modeller, nor even for an experienced modeller unless they have experience in vacuform modelling, and preferably in building very large vacuform kits. Nonetheless, this kit can be made into a show-stopping model, as is seen in the following build.

The aircraft itself, the Handley Page Halifax, was designed to meet the same specifications that produced the Avro Manchester, the disappointing progenitor of the famous Lancaster. The designers of the Halifax wisely switched from utilising two of the troublesome Vulture engines to four of the fine Merlins. Thus, the Halifax never went through an intermediate two-engined version as the Lancaster did (with the Manchester), but entered service as a four-engined bomber, the second of the modern RAF four-engined heavy bombers, after the Short Stirling.

1/32 scale Handley Page Halifax GR.II, Tigger Models Vacuform
by Tom Probert

I've always had a bit of a soft spot for the Halifax; the venerable 'Halibag' forever seems to be in the shadow of the mighty Lancaster. Not only did the Halifax give gallant service in Bomber Command throughout the Second World War, it also served with distinction in Transport Command and Coastal Command, and although its early career was hindered by under-performance and stability issues, it went on to become a stalwart as one of the RAF's 'heavies'.

Modellers have had the option of replicating the Halifax in model form for many a year. The classic Bristol Hercules-powered 1/72 scale Airfix kit has been around since the 1960s, later to be joined by a Rolls-Royce Merlin version from Matchbox in the 1970s. Revell then released both Hercules and Merlin versions in the mid-2000s.

The 1/48 scale has been less well catered for, with the Contrail vacuforms (later produced by Sanger) being the only options until Fonderie released their Mk III in the late 1990s. Unsurprisingly, manufacturers have tended to steer away from 1/32 scale kits of four-engined bombers due to their sheer size and cost. Currently, Hong Kong Models have bucked the trend, having released a 1/32 scale Avro Lancaster, which follows the release of their B-17. When I was planning to build a Halifax, the only option of a kit in 1/32 scale was (and, at the time of writing, still is) the Tigger Models' vacuform, which is based on the old ID Models moulds produced in the late 1970s and early 1980s. Both Hercules and Merlin variants were produced, but currently only the Rolls-Royce engine version is in production.

Often, when you mention the word 'vacuform' to a fellow modeller, they tend to lose colour rapidly and start to quiver. The prospect of cutting out and preparing the parts before assembly is seen as a chore by those who tend to build models purely for relaxation. Then, having to spend many hours scratchbuilding parts is enough to push many over the edge—especially when combined with the soft detailing and lack of surface detail often characteristic of vacuform kits. However, I have never been one to shy away from a modelling challenge, and therefore I decided that if I was going to build a Halifax, I was going to do it properly. I promptly ordered a kit from Tigger Models.

When the kit arrived, the sheer size of it struck me—this was going to be a long and complex project. The shapes of the airframe seemed reasonably accurate, but there was no interior, undercarriage, propellers, or any other detailed parts provided. In short, you are provided with a 'shell', which forms a blank canvas for the modeller to work their magic. This next picture shows how the parts arrive, with the fuselage halves still in their backing sheet, which will, of course, need to be removed before construction can begin.

Basic vacuforms such as these are devoid of surface detail. I consider this a good thing as due to the nature of the moulding process, panel lines can be soft, and therefore I prefer to scribe my own. Good plans are essential for this, and although total accuracy is not my greatest concern, I do like the finished model to be a reasonable representation of the real aircraft. 1/72 scale Halifax plans from Aerodata International were sourced and enlarged to 1/32 scale, and I duly set about adding the panel detail. For the larger parts, I did this while the part was still in the backing sheet as this

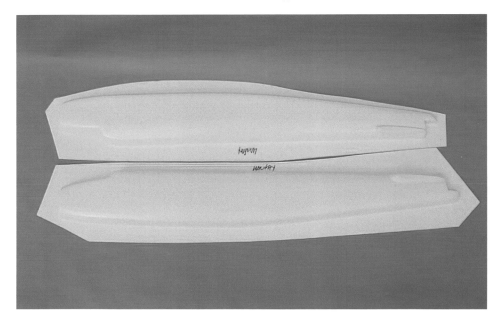

Halifax fuselage halves before being cut out of the backing sheet. (*Tom Probert*)

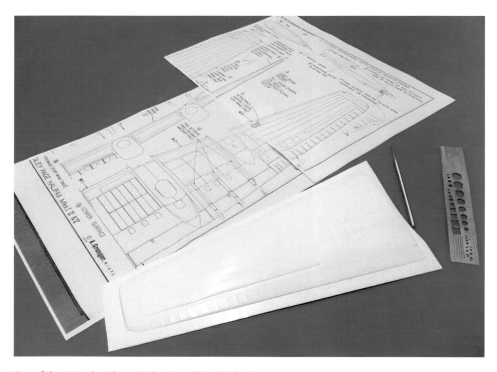

One of the wings beside scale drawings. (*Tom Probert*)

kept it stable and reduced flexing, and thus greatly reduced the risk of the scriber slipping.

There are various ways to remove the individual parts. My preferred method is to score around the part with a new No. 11 blade at a 45-degree angle, and then to break the part from the backing sheet. I then remove any excess plastic by sanding the part on a flat sheet of wet and dry paper, until the correct thickness is achieved. Regular checking of the plans is a must. It is imperative to take your time here, as removing too much plastic is hard to correct—it's far easier removing excess plastic when the time comes rather than trying to add it back again.

When building a model of this size and nature, I usually start with the wings as this enables me to build a very strong spar structure to help keep the model rigid early in the process. I use 1-mm plastic card sheet, and with a profile gauge, cut accurate internal bracing and spars. I glue them firmly to the underside of the wing interior using polystyrene cement. This creates a very strong bond between the plastics—stronger, after twenty-four hours of drying, than the bond achieved with CA glue.

The Tigger kit has the inner and outer wing sections moulded separately, so work began on the inner sections, which contained the three bomb bays within the wing. I decided to have these displayed open, so set about making the bays themselves, as well as the internal structure that separates the bomb cells. The undercarriage bays were also constructed at this point, which entailed making the forward spars, firewalls, and

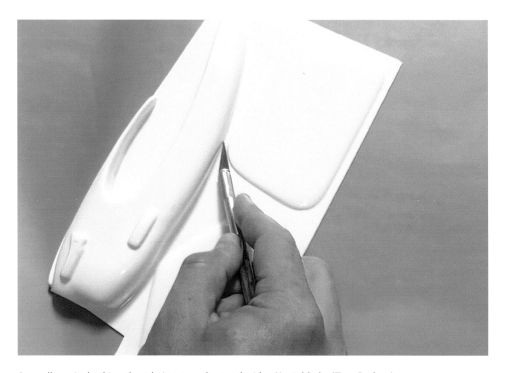

A nacelle on its backing sheet being scored around with a No. 11 blade. (*Tom Probert*)

rear bulkheads. I did not add any of the finer details at this point as there was a danger of them being damaged—they would come later when the wing was structurally complete. The next picture gives an idea of the internal bracing required.

The outer wing sections followed the same pattern, with plenty of internal bracing being fitted. When the upper and lower wing halves had been glued together, they were attached to the inner wing section with the help of interlocking spars, this time made from 2-mm plastic card for additional strength. Careful checking of the plans was necessary to get the correct dihedral. With the inner and outer sections of the wings together, I added any surface details that had been obliterated by sanding and filling.

With the main structure of the wings complete, I turned my attention to the engine nacelles. The kit captures the shape of the streamlined Rolls-Royce Merlin nacelle accurately, but the exhaust and carburettor intake detail was very soft and needed removing. These apertures were banked with plastic card in preparation for scratchbuilt replacements to be added later in the build.

The inlets for the radiators were opened up with a sharp blade and the basic radiator front detail was replicated using plastic card and a fine wire mesh. With this complete and installed into the front of the nacelles, the interior was sprayed matt black and the two halves were joined. It was at this point that I decided to add some extra visual detail to this project. I removed the number two nacelle at the firewall to have the engine and all of its associated plumbing and bearers exposed. With the construction of the nacelles completed, they were attached to the wing; the upper fairings took a lot of careful measuring and cutting to get a respectable fit. Automotive filler was used to blend everything in, and then the panel detail and cowling fasteners were added with a scriber and a 0.5-mm drill. At this point I also began to add some of the internal detail to the main landing gear bays, as handling the wings when attached to the fuselage would be quite challenging.

With the wings completed, I felt they looked a little bland in this impressive scale, so I decided to remove the flaps and display them dropped (as seen on parked Halifaxes). I also opted to open the dinghy stowage panel and build the interior. On the upper forward part of the inner wing, I opened the wing bomb bay winching holes to add a little more interest to this area, as well as to let a little more light into the bays themselves.

With the wings set aside, work could begin on the fuselage. Following the plans carefully, all the windows were removed, as well as the opening for the bomb bay, and the panel detail was scribed. With no interior parts available, the whole interior had to be made from scratch, but as only the flightdeck and nose section were visible, the workload was not as great as it might have been. Again, plastic card and Evergreen strip provided the material to recreate the interior. A following picture shows the work in progress.

I'm not a modeller who wishes to recreate every tiny detail, but using numerous reference pictures, a reasonable representation of the forward fuselage could be made. Some careful airbrushing and a little light weathering meant that, when peering through the canopy, the level of detail was passable.

With the necessary internal details complete, the fuselage halves were joined using plastic tabs along the mating surfaces to obtain extra strength. Additional bulkheads were made throughout the length of the fuselage, and the roof to the bomb bay was

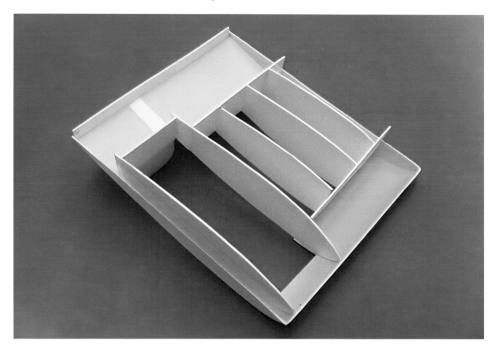

The inner wing with landing gear wells and bomb bays boxed off with sheet plastic. (*Tom Probert*)

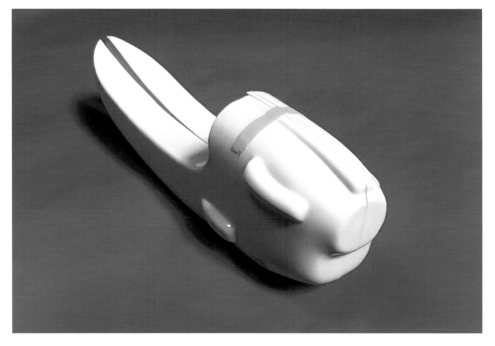

The nacelle taped together to check the fit. (*Tom Probert*)

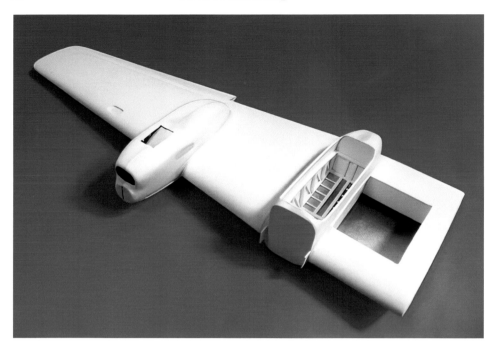

Bottom of the port wing, but without the inboard engine and wing bomb bays attached. (*Tom Probert*)

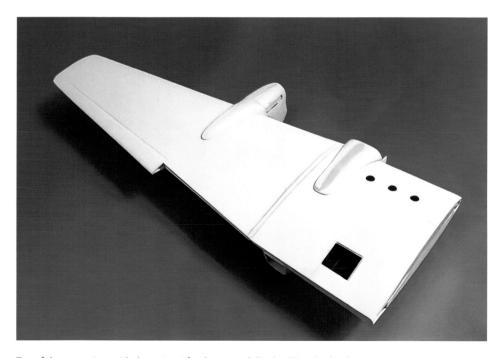

Top of the port wing, with the cut-out for the stowed dinghy. (*Tom Probert*)

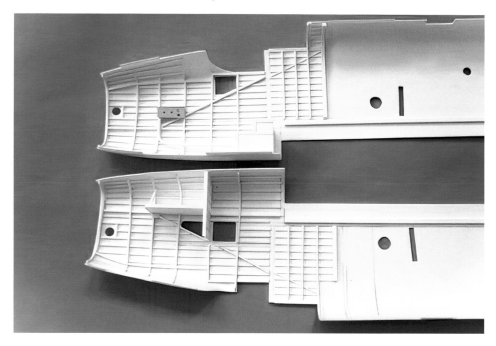

Fuselage interiors, with plastic strips added to the cockpit section to increase detail. (*Tom Probert*)

The fuselage interior built up and painted. Most of this has been scratchbuilt. (*Tom Probert*)

made and fitted. The fit of the fuselage halves was reasonable, but more automotive filler and a session with some wet and dry paper ensured that all traces of the join were removed. Once again, any panel detail damaged by the sanding process was repaired, and I could now think about joining the wings to the fuselage. This was done with the aid of wooden dowels, which formed strong spars that slid into the wing structure and created a good, solid join between the fuselage and wings.

With the wings now attached to the fuselage, I could turn my attention to the stabilisers and fins. Detail on both the twin rudders and elevators was poor, and with the shape of the stabilisers and elevators being incorrect, I decided to scratchbuild my own elevators and rudders from plastic card. Panel detail was scribed on, and the hinges were made from Evergreen strip.

The fins and stabilisers, along with the homemade rudders and elevators, were then attached to the model. The joins were blended with more filler. At this point I also finished off the rear fuselage by making the fairing for the rear turret, as this was missing in the kit.

With the Halifax now structurally complete, I could now concentrate on adding the finer details to the model, all of which needed to be made from scratch. I began by replicating the bomb bay structure, a complex maze of cross members and bracing. Each would need to be measured and made individually, including the drilling out of numerous lightening holes, as seen on the real aircraft. This took a number of evenings, but with careful consultation of my references, the basic bomb bay structure was completed. More details such as pipework and wring would be added later, along with scratchbuilt bomb racks and, of course, the complex door structure.

The huge Messier undercarriage also had to be made from scratch, but due to its boxy and robust structure, it was relatively simple to construct from plastic card, along with a few smaller details which came from the spares box. The wheels themselves were resin items, kindly produced by a fellow modeller who also builds large-scale vacuforms. I was thus saved a lot of extra work.

The retraction mechanisms were also made from plastic card. These were test-fitted to the main struts to check the sit of the model, and thankfully everything sat level and correct; no further work on the gear was needed prior to installation just before the painting process. The tail wheel was made from a modified spare 1/72 scale Avro Lancaster mainwheel, along with other various items from the spares box. The large H2S radar blister was also mated to the fuselage, and detail was added to the wing bomb bays from more Evergreen strip.

With the model now nearing the painting stage, I made and added the final details to the cockpit. An Eduard seat harness was added to the pilot's seat, but all other details were scratchbuilt. The flat side windows were made from plastic strip as these were poorly represented by the kit parts. The glazing for these side panels was added later in the form of clear acetate, which was cut to the correct size and dropped into the apertures.

Propellers were the next hurdle. With none provided in the kit and no after-market parts available, these too had to be handmade. By this point I had decided to replicate a Coastal Command Halifax. These aircraft were fitted with up-rated Merlin XXs and four-bladed propellers. I had some spare 1/24 scale de Havilland Mosquito blades, so I

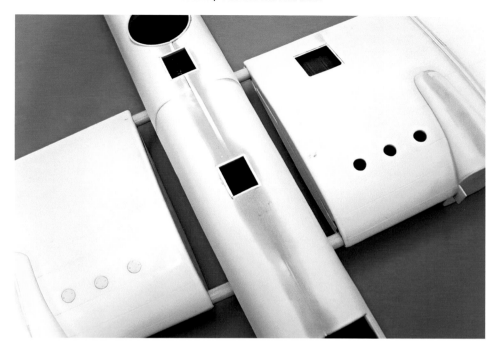

Wings showing how they attach to the fuselage using wooden dowels for strength. (*Tom Probert*)

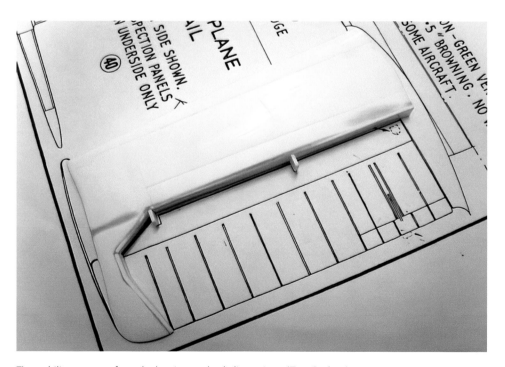

The stabiliser on top of a scale drawing to check dimensions. (*Tom Probert*)

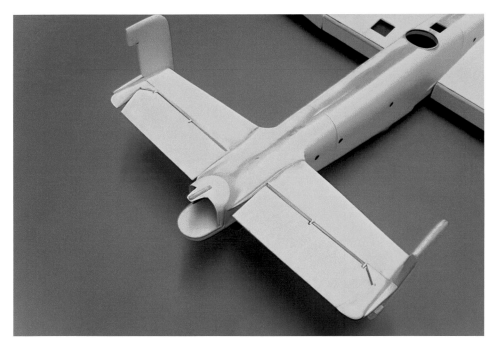

The rear turret fairing and tail planes, complete except for the rudders. (*Tom Probert*)

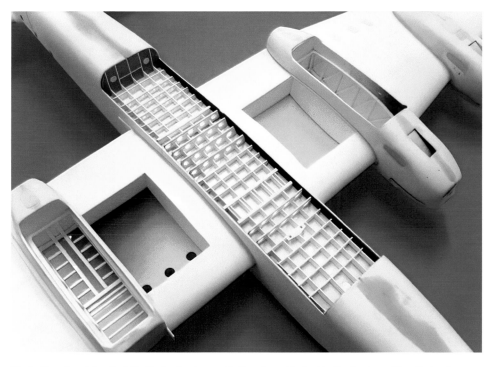

The built-up bomb bay installed in the fuselage, with the wings attached to the fuselage. (*Tom Probert*)

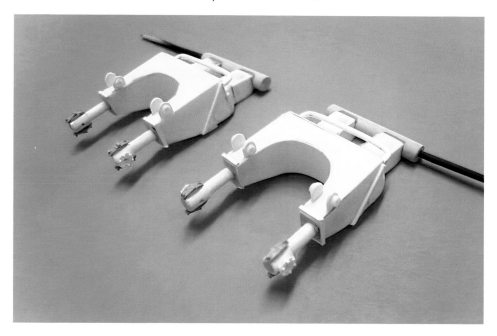

The scratchbuilt main landing gear legs. (*Tom Probert*)

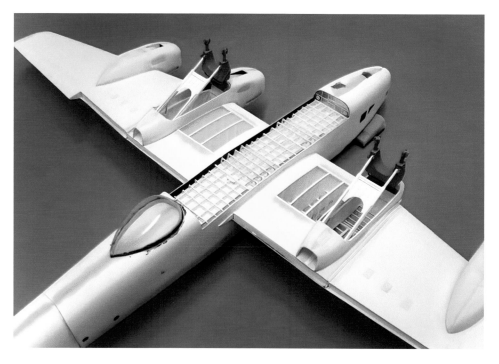

The model is nearly complete, with landing gear installed and the large, clear H2S radome glued onto the fuselage. (*Tom Probert*)

The cockpit in place in the glued-together fuselage. (*Tom Probert*)

modified one to the correct shape for the Halifax and had them cast in resin. I did the same for the carburettor intakes; a master was made and then they too were resin cast. The spinners were made by plunge-moulding a Milliput master, with the blades being fitted to a backing plate before installation on the engine fronts. With the number two engine being exposed, I modelled the blades in the fully feathered position.

The kit comes with a crystal clear vacuformed cockpit transparency, and with some careful trimming, it fitted the fuselage well. The internal framing was made from plastic strip and off-cuts of sprue, and was painted and installed before the glazing itself was placed over the top. Some filler was needed to blend everything in, and when completed, the canopy was masked in preparation for painting. I also added the final smaller details at this point, such as the de-icer jets, balance horns on the ailerons, the DF-loop (from Milliput), and various other smaller external details.

By this stage I had decided on a final paint scheme. As the more powerful and generally better Halifax Mk IIIs came into service, the older Merlin-powered machines were transferred into Coastal Command. When researching which aircraft to replicate I came across a number of these Mk II Halifaxes that were transferred. Most were repainted into the Coastal Command colour scheme, but a number retained their Bomber Command scheme, but with the dull red codes replaced by grey ones. JP328 was one of these unusual examples; it really interested me and so I chose to replicate it. With the 58 Squadron codes painted grey and masked off, along with the wing roundels, I set about

The forward fuselage with the cockpit canopy now glued into place. (*Tom Probert*)

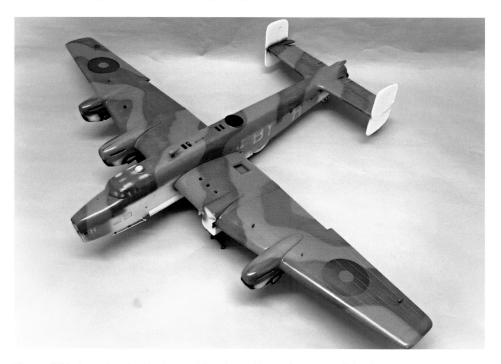

The model being painted with the topside colours. Notice that some of the decals have already been applied. (*Tom Probert*)

applying the standard Bomber Command camouflage pattern of dark green/dark earth to the upper surfaces.

With the upper surfaces masked off, night black was applied to the lower surfaces. I then did some subtle post-shading of the upper colours (I kept the weathering of the black to the absolute minimum as shown in contemporary pictures) and applied the fuselage roundels (spares box) as well as the serial number and fin-flashes (Xtradecal) to complete the painting process.

With the painting process complete, I continued to add the finer details to the model. There were no turret interiors provided in the kit, so contemporary pictures were consulted, and I scratchbuilt the internal structures. The guns themselves were Aires examples, with ammunition belts coming from Eduard. Both the rear and mid-upper turrets were crash-moulded over Milliput masters (the kit turrets were the wrong shape) and these were then added to their respective apertures before the painted transparencies were glued into position. Finally, brass barrels were added from Master—a must in this scale.

The exposed number two engine was tackled next. I contacted Tamiya and purchased a sprue from their excellent Spitfire kit and set about backdating the engine to a single-stage supercharged Merlin XX. The firewall was made from plastic card, and the engine mountings and cooling system were all heavily modified Tamiya parts. Some extra wiring and piping was added, and the engine was then attached to the nacelle.

My attention then returned once again to the bomb bay: piping, hydraulic lines, and scratchbuilt bomb racks were all painted and weathered, and then added to the bays. The bomb doors and actuating mechanisms were all scratchbuilt from plastic card and Evergreen strip, and glued into the open position.

I was now on the home straight. After making my own exhausts, the propellers were painted, weathered lightly, and glued in place.

The final task was to add the nose transparency. The kit part was used, but this also required the internal bracing to be made (from Evergreen) for the .50-calibre machine gun, which was fitted to Coastal Command Halifaxes. The gun and barrel were both from Aires.

Finally, after ten months of work, I had a 1/32 scale Halifax to add to my collection.

The detailed bomb bays and main landing gear are now painted, along with the underside of the model. (*Tom Probert*)

The mid-upper (dorsal) turret position showing detail of the guns and their mounts. (*Tom Probert*)

The detailed Merlin engine, to be attached to the port inboard nacelle. (*Tom Probert*)

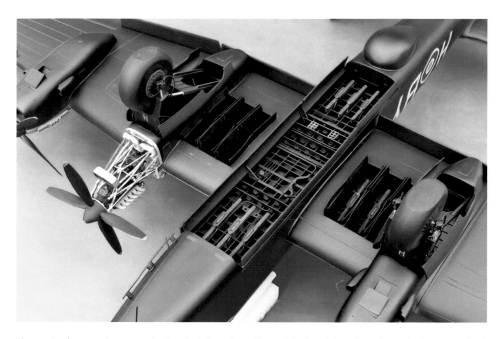

The engine has now been attached to the inboard nacelle, and the bomb bay doors have also been attached. Note the flattened bottoms of the main wheels. (*Tom Probert*)

The finished engine nacelles with exhaust stains applied. (*Tom Probert*)

The finished model from the front, showing the front gun position. (*Tom Probert*)

The finished model from the back, showing the lowered flaps and the open dinghy storage compartment in the inboard portion of the port wing. (*Tom Probert*)

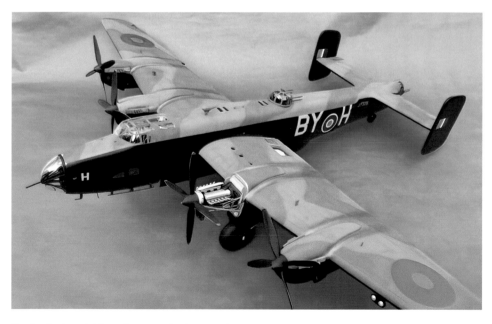

The finished model from the port side, showing the exposed inboard port engine. The propellers have been 'feathered'. (*Tom Probert*)

3
Scratchbuilding

AN INTRODUCTION BY CLAUDIO LUCHINA

For some more obscure aircraft, modelling kits, whether injection-moulded, resin, or vacuform, do not exist. In these cases, scratchbuilding the model—in effect, creating the 'kit' yourself—comes into play. The intention of the following pages is to provide a brief but hopefully helpful introduction to the field of scratchbuilding.

Think of scratchbuilding as a means of expanding your understanding of both the aircraft you are modelling and the art of modelling itself. On a practical level, it will help improve your manual dexterity and modelling skills. You will learn new techniques and how to use new materials, and will discover new facts about the history of the plane you are modelling. It's also fun and exciting, and given that any subject can be scratchbuilt, it will widen immensely your modelling horizons. General ideas and procedures will be discussed in this chapter, and examples presented to ignite your passion for this aspect of the hobby we all share and love.

Scratchbuilding, like most things, is easy once you have learned how to do it. Like building commercial kits, once you have acquired the necessary skills and knowledge, a whole universe of potential subjects will be opened to you. Imagine being able to build whatever plane you want, in the scale you want, with the level of detail you want, for a reasonable price. Yes, it requires time, patience, and persistence, just like 'normal' modelling—no less, no more.

There are a number of extremely talented scratchbuilders out there; look at their work and learn as much as you can. My path is to pursue techniques that are as simple as possible and relatively fast to complete, so scratchbuilding a model takes little more, about the same, or even less time than building a commercial kit (especially when commercial kits require a great deal of refining or alteration given their low standard). With that approach I have been able to produce a large number of scratchbuilt models and to modify existing kits with this or that scratchbuilt detail. But it's not about numbers, it's about fun and what gives you pleasure.

The Parts of the Process

SELECTING A SUITABLE SUBJECT FOR A SCRATCHBUILDING PROJECT

When choosing a subject you should consider a simple design with reasonable documentation (including a plan or three-view and photos) and a small number of parts of easy fabrication and assembly. An attractive but overly complex subject will present a lot of challenges for a first step into scratchbuilding. The chosen aircraft should, however, be attractive enough to keep you motivated through the different stages of the build.

Think of your first scratch effort as a sort of exercise, and not the means of immediately creating a superlative modelling jewel. Small steps and reasonable expectations should characterise your approach to the task at hand. The first project will serve as a test bank to familiarise yourself with scratchbuilding, but before you venture forth, it is highly advisable that you are proficient in the making of conventional kits, and have some experience in kit modification or building vacuformed kits. It is also helpful if you have dabbled in paper or balsa modelling, as methods and techniques overlap.

Essentially, if you have already detailed a commercial kit, or even better, have modified one to a comprehensive degree, you should be ready for the next step.

PREPARATIONS

The first step in scratchbuilding is gathering reference material from any source you can: books, magazines, the internet, etc. I have occasionally used my local public library to good effect when I could not afford or was unable to access a particular publication. A plan or three-view will be indispensable, and if none can be found, one will have to be made (but later, for more advanced projects).

A reasonable set of modelling tools and supplies, especially styrene rods, strips, sticks, and sheets, is a must. To have access to a small vacuforming machine (like a Mattel) would make life wonderful and be useful for many years of joyful modelling (as mine has been!). A well-stocked spares bin is also a blessing, but there are many aftermarket suppliers that sell accessories such as engines, wheels, propellers, seats, and the like. Everything can be fabricated, but it saves time and energy to get some things already made where possible.

STARTING

The plan or three-view has to be sized to the scale intended (1/72 in my case) and printed. I use heavy paper stock. The different parts have to be transferred to the desired material (styrene sheet mostly in this case) of adequate thickness (.010, .015, .020, etc., depending on size, type of part—flying surface, fuselage sides, etc.—and scale).

ENGINEERING

A number of different approaches and techniques are used for scratchbuilding. Because of my modelling background, I tend to combine those used in flying balsa models, paper models and even full-scale aviation engineering, besides those normally used with commercial models. Each modeller, after experimenting, will find what works for them, and eventually find new techniques or modify existing ones to solve engineering or fabrication challenges. Think of the process as first producing a kit, and then assembling it. Flexibility, resourcefulness and ingenuity are desirable traits, and will be enhanced as you scratchbuild your first projects.

Needless to say, making scale models requires a degree of accuracy in representing the original aircraft, but for first-time scratchbuilders it is suggested that the accuracy of internal and external details, and to some extent measurements, should be pursued to a fair, but not obsessive degree. The first scratch models should be thought of as a training ground for more complex future projects. The golden rule is to keep it simple.

Scratchbuilding is a natural consequence of the tendency in some modellers to add or correct detail on existing kits. It is also born of the need to represent types neglected by manufacturers. In fact, before the industry provided kits—very recently in historical terms—*all* modellers were scratchbuilders.

Scratchbuilding is not necessarily more complicated or time-consuming than building a challenging kit. Experienced modellers will often spend many hours correcting, adding, or replacing parts on their models. Scratchbuilding also does not require many more tools and supplies than those usually found on a well-equipped modelling bench. Plastic sheets, rods and sticks usually form the base of scratchbuilt models, and wood (generally basswood or balsa) and metal (in the form of wire, tube, and foil) usually complete the materials used.

Keeping the balance between the challenge and the satisfaction of a positive outcome is a real art, and therefore your first scratch projects should be kept as simple as possible so they can be taken to the finish line without major complications. The whole experience is not necessarily a stairway to heaven, and often many attempts are required to get things right, especially at the beginning as new techniques and materials are tried for the first time.

As said above, the project begins with the subject choice and research stage, whereby all the information needed to make an accurate replica is gathered: plans and three-views, photos, articles, and the like. I have a very small aviation library, so I usually find all I need for a given modelling project on the virtual cornucopia that is the internet.

The following builds are intended to provide some broad sense of the techniques, materials, and sequences used in scratchbuilding. I hope they awaken your sense of adventure in the art of modelling.

Aircraft Modelling

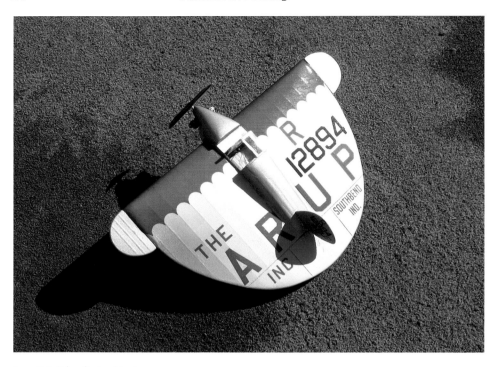

Arup S-2. (*Claudio Luchina*)

Capelis. (*Claudio Luchina*)

Curtiss-Cox Wildcat. (*Claudio Luchina*)

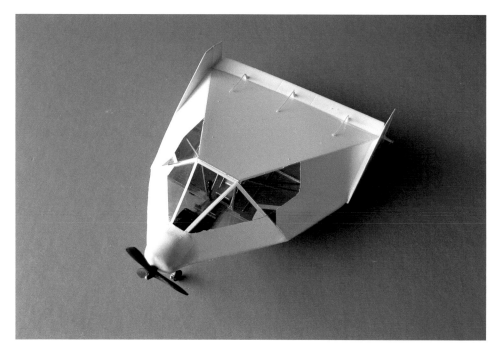

Facetmobile. (*Claudio Luchina*)

Granger Archaeopterix. (*Claudio Luchina*)

Nieuport Japanese Experimental. (*Claudio Luchina*)

Riout Alerion. (*Claudio Luchina*)

Rocheville Arctic Tern. (*Claudio Luchina*)

HENDERSON-GLENNY GADFLY (I, II AND III)

The smallish Gadfly I started life in 1929 as an ABC Scorpion-powered conventional monoplane of simple lines and conservative design. Soon afterwards, its ailerons were deleted and a new device was installed: the so-called 'oyster' rotary ailerons. This aircraft became the Gadfly II. The Gadfly III had a Salmson 9AD radial. Given its rectangular wing and stabilizer, and its uncomplicated fuselage and details, this rather simple, small and conventional subject is ideal for an entry-level scratchbuilding project.

I happened to have an old Aeroclub Salmson 9AD white metal engine, so I built the Gadfly III (G-AARK), which had that engine. Photographs can be found of it flying with both 'oyster' and normal ailerons, but I used the 'oyster' ones since I had never seen them on a model. The techniques and resources I used for this build are not written in stone, and there are many ways to solve scratchbuilding engineering challenges. The build is only meant to be indicative of some basic approaches to the task.

It is rightly said that an image is worth a thousand words, so we should let the images of the building steps show how it was done. Pay attention to materials and tools, as well as the engineering approaches. And again, these are suggestions, not rigid methods.

Styrene sheet is used for making flying surfaces. Depending on the scale and size, .010-, .015-, .020-inch, and so on is used. One way to obtain a mild curvature is to roll a dowel or tube on the sheet, preferably trapped between two sheets of thick paper to avoid leaving marks. (*Claudio Luchina*)

As you can see, the technique is sometimes similar to the one used for paper models. The top part of the surface can be bent over the bottom (using a spar) and glued at the trailing edge. (*Claudio Luchina*)

A flat surface is needed to protect against warping. (*Claudio Luchina*)

Here, wing and tail elements are ready, and construction of the fuselage begins, very much like some balsa models. (*Claudio Luchina*)

Sheeting of the fuselage ensues. The bottom is secured first. A piece of styrene is glued, and once the glue dries, the bottom is trimmed until the fuselage sides are reached. You must check for symmetry. (*Claudio Luchina*)

Strips are glued from inside the fuselage to secure the curved top sections later on. (*Claudio Luchina*)

Simple seats can be built easily. (*Claudio Luchina*)

The top sections of the fuselage have been measured, cut, curved, and glued on. Time to raid the spares box and see if you can find something useful (wheels, props, engines, P.E. parts). Otherwise, some parts may be obtained from aftermarket vendors. (*Claudio Luchina*)

Before adding the top section for the cockpit, the interior needs to be addressed. (*Claudio Luchina*)

The fuselage is ready. Continue to check for symmetry and alignment. (*Claudio Luchina*)

Time to make the landing gear. Here you can use wire, flattened wire, or if you are lucky, some aero-foiled material like Strutz or Contrail (which is no longer produced). (*Claudio Luchina*)

The main elements are glued together. Notice the metal horns on the elevators, cut from discarded aluminium containers and lids (the top of a soda bottle will do), which are both thin and sturdy. (*Claudio Luchina*)

Consider the other elements to be added, and work out a sequence for painting and detailing. (*Claudio Luchina*)

The painted model without decals, but with the control cables and engine installed. (*Claudio Luchina*)

A small model, but great fun. (*Claudio Luchina*)

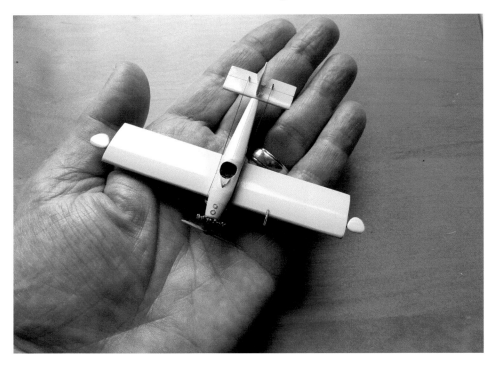

The completed model without decals. (*Claudio Luchina*)

The completed model with decals from the front. (*Claudio Luchina*)

The completed model from the top and port side. (*Claudio Luchina*)

The completed model from the top and starboard side. (*Claudio Luchina*)

The completed model 'in flight'. (*Claudio Luchina*)

FARMAN F.21 MOUSTIQUE II, 1924 TOUR DE FRANCE DES AVIONETTES

Being a simple, squarish design, the Farman F.21 Moustique II is another suitable candidate for scratchbuilding. It also has some extra details to make it more interesting. The building process involves rigging, masking, and detailing: nothing you have not already done before if you are a kit builder of some experience.

Styrene sheet is used, this time lightly embossed with a ballpoint pen from the inside. The embossing is done over a piece of cardboard or several sheets of discarded paper. Consistency is an art to be developed by practice. (*Claudio Luchina*)

The inner surface of the sheet is first drawn as a guide for the embossing. (*Claudio Luchina*)

The spar in place, both surfaces were pre-curved. (*Claudio Luchina*)

The same was done for the tail surfaces. (*Claudio Luchina*)

The aerofoil is made. (*Claudio Luchina*)

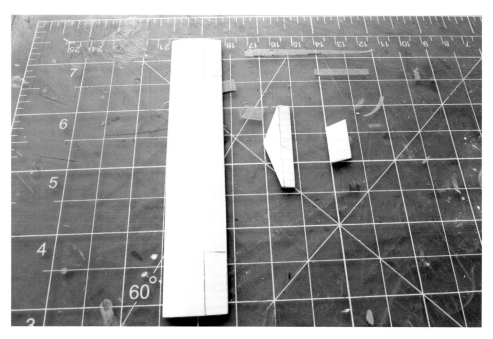

All flying surfaces are ready. The elevator and aileron lines are engraved with the proper tool. I use the Olfa brand with the blade that looks a bit like a hook. (*Claudio Luchina*)

The fuselage, a simple box, follows the same procedure as that of the previous model, similar to making balsa fuselages for flying models. (*Claudio Luchina*)

All the main parts are ready. (*Claudio Luchina*)

Time to look for those accessories in the spares bin, or to get them from aftermarket suppliers. (*Claudio Luchina*)

The ends of the wingtips need capping. (*Claudio Luchina*)

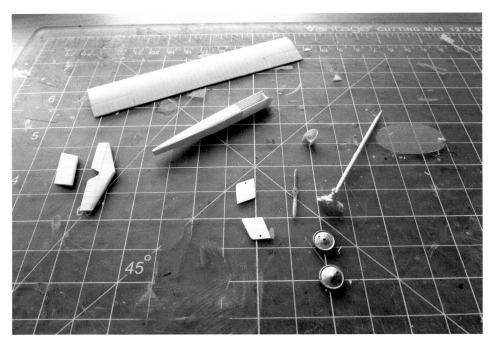

All parts are accounted for. (*Claudio Luchina*)

The wing tip capped. (*Claudio Luchina*)

The interior is put in place before that area is covered. (*Claudio Luchina*)

The spars and front of the fuselage. (*Claudio Luchina*)

The wing is glued on. (*Claudio Luchina*)

The front of the fuselage and headrest are adjusted for a good fit. (*Claudio Luchina*)

The tail post, metal control horns (there are photoetched ones available), and landing gear are in place. (*Claudio Luchina*)

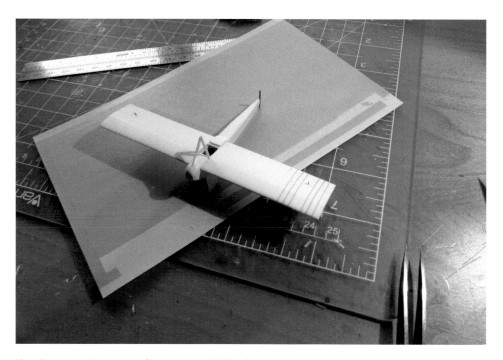

The rib tapes in the process of being masked. (*Claudio Luchina*)

All the rib tapes are now masked. (*Claudio Luchina*)

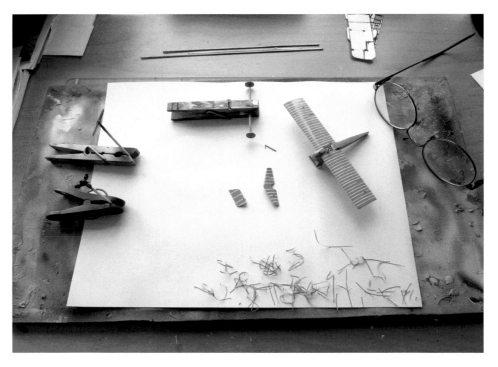

Paint is applied and the masks are removed. (*Claudio Luchina*)

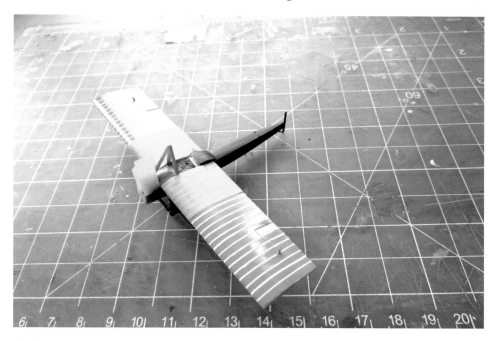

The fuselage is painted wood, with a light colour acrylic base and oil washes. (*Claudio Luchina*)

The completed model from the top. (*Claudio Luchina*)

The completed model from the top and port side. (*Claudio Luchina*)

The completed model from the top and starboard side. (*Claudio Luchina*)

The completed model from the top and aft. (*Claudio Luchina*)

The completed model from the top and starboard side. (*Claudio Luchina*)

The completed model from the top and forward. (*Claudio Luchina*)

The completed model from beneath. (*Claudio Luchina*)

LATÉCOÈRE L.A.T.8 OR LATE 8

This was an early medium-sized attempt at a passenger/postal carrier, designed to fly short routes with less demand. In many ways, it resembles the later and much more successful Breguet 14T 'cabine', which was used in the same way.

The Late 8 could carry five passengers and included the luxury of a restroom equipped with a toilet, which was proudly announced in contemporary advertisements. The pilot, as with many other designs of the time, sat quite far back in an exposed cockpit on the fuselage, to the right of the spine, and had to access his position from the exterior. Photographs show some changes in inscriptions and details during the aircraft's life.

This model is an example of a more complex scratchbuilding project, requiring additional skills, but without presenting any insurmountable challenges. The Late 8 is bigger than the Farman and Gadfly, has a passenger cabin with details, and the fuselage involves windows and surface detail, and requires more parts and more engineering.

Other complexities, like rigging and dealing with a biplane configuration, painting, and such, are all issues also present in building commercial kits, so hopefully the builder may have acquired the necessary experience long before attempting a complex scratchbuilding project.

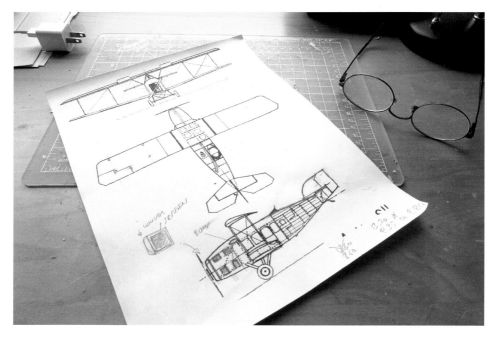

Always study the documentation and check it, where possible, against photos (no plan is perfect), and make the necessary corrections. Devise a sound engineering and building strategy. (*Claudio Luchina*)

Embossed tail surfaces with spars added. (*Claudio Luchina*)

The side of the fuselage will be made of styrene sheet slabs. Fuselage sides, tops and bottoms require sturdier styrene than the flying surfaces, depending on scale and size: .020-, .030-, .040-inch, and so forth. (*Claudio Luchina*)

Wing skins being prepared. (*Claudio Luchina*)

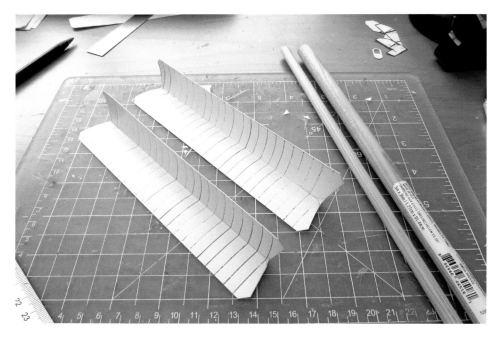

Curvature is induced while using light cardboard on the top and bottom of the styrene sheet to avoid marks being left by the dowels or tubes used to imprint the curvature. (*Claudio Luchina*)

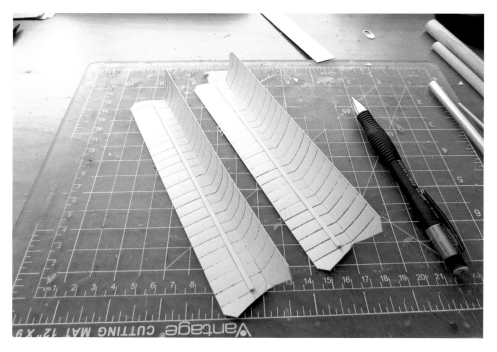

The spars in place. (*Claudio Luchina*)

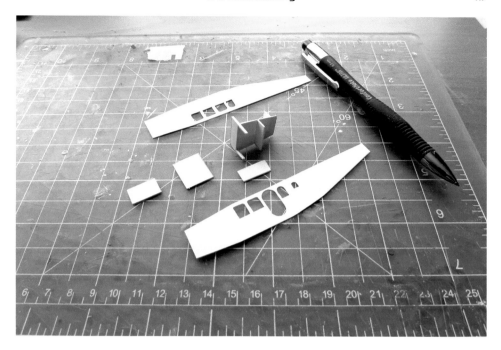

The interior being built. (*Claudio Luchina*)

Examples of other seats made from scratch. (*Claudio Luchina*)

The seats for this model. (*Claudio Luchina*)

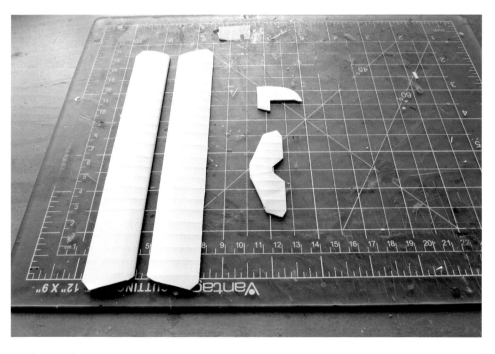

The flying surfaces ready. (*Claudio Luchina*)

The inner structure for the saddle wing tanks is prepared. (*Claudio Luchina*)

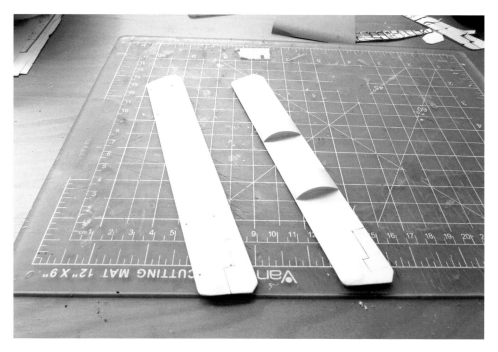

The saddle tanks are skinned and glued on. (*Claudio Luchina*)

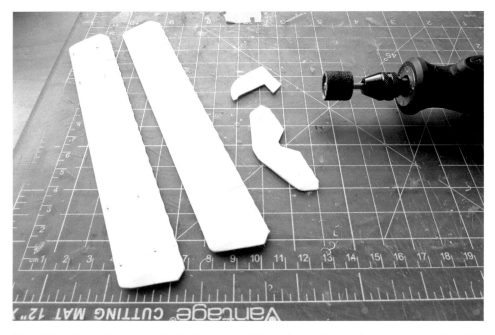

The trailing edge scallops are made with the very careful use of a rotating sanding drum and sanding stick. (*Claudio Luchina*)

The propeller is carved from wood. (*Claudio Luchina*)

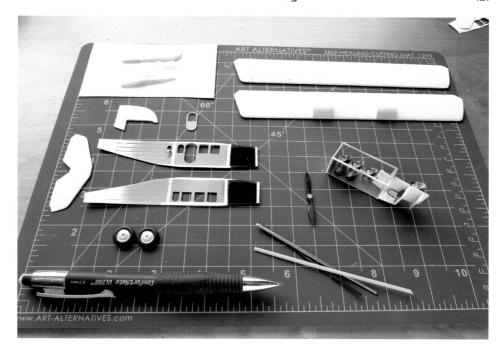

Some painting. (*Claudio Luchina*)

A view of the interior. (*Claudio Luchina*)

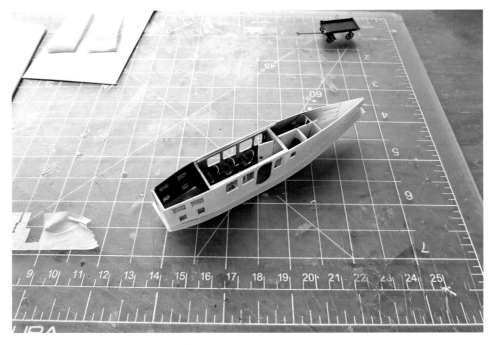

The fuselage is assembled. (*Claudio Luchina*)

An engine is fabricated. Just the basic shapes, as it will be almost completely hidden. (*Claudio Luchina*)

The nose is vacuformed on a secondhand commercial machine (now discontinued). (*Claudio Luchina*)

The wooden master and the part. (*Claudio Luchina*)

Covering in sections of the top fuselage. The stringers are embossed from inside on the aft section. (*Claudio Luchina*)

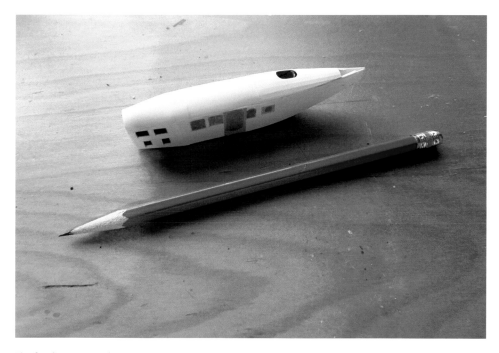

The fuselage is completed prior to the lower wing being attached. (*Claudio Luchina*)

The very long exhaust is made carefully by heating and bending a length of styrene tube. At the top of the picture is the lower wing, now attached to the fuselage. (*Claudio Luchina*)

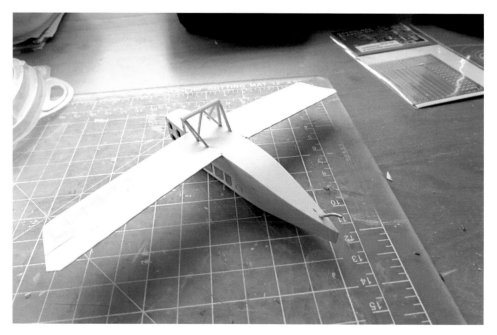

The landing gear is in place. Aero-foiled stock from Contrail and Strutz (now discontinued) has been used here, but flattened wire or shaped styrene sticks could also be used. (*Claudio Luchina*)

After the application of aluminium paint over a black coat, struts and ancillary parts are glued in place. (*Claudio Luchina*)

The upper wing is attached, and the rigging is next. (*Claudio Luchina*)

The rigging done, the model is complete. Here it is from the top, front, and starboard. (*Claudio Luchina*)

The completed model from the top and starboard. (*Claudio Luchina*)

The completed model from the front and starboard. (*Claudio Luchina*)

The completed model from ground level and starboard. (*Claudio Luchina*)

The completed model from ground level, front, and starboard. (*Claudio Luchina*)

The completed model from ground level, front, and port. (*Claudio Luchina*)

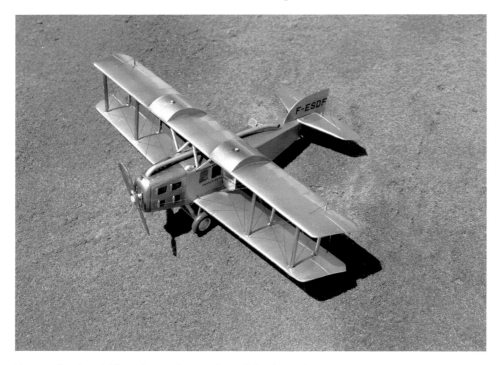

The completed model from the top, front, and port. (*Claudio Luchina*)

The completed model from the top, back, and starboard. (*Claudio Luchina*)

The completed model 'in flight'. (*Claudio Luchina*)

Closing words

The more you build, the more you learn, the more able you become and the faster you become. But this is not a race; it's about enjoyment and learning new skills. Still, modellers with limited time can appreciate simple techniques and practical building and engineering strategies.

But one size does not fit all. You must explore, practice, adapt and recreate in order to find the techniques that suit you, keeping the levels of challenge, skill and enjoyment in balanced proportions. So get at it with a joyful mood, willing to learn from the mistakes. Each one of them is a path to betterment.

4
Superdetailing

Although injection-moulded kits have come a very long way from their early beginnings in terms of external and internal detailing, there are times when you wish to add a little (or a lot) more detail. This extra detailing often creates a far more accurate representation of the original aircraft as well as making the model more interesting to look at. It can change a good model into an excellent model, even a contest winner. This is where superdetailing comes in. With the huge number of aftermarket resin and photoetched detailing sets currently available for many different kits in different scales, some level of superdetailing is now well within the means of even the average modeller. Of course, much superdetailing can also be done with scratchbuilding, or a combination of aftermarket sets and scratchbuilding.

1/72 SCALE FAIREY FIREFLY

The Fairey Fulmar two-seat shipborne fighter proved to be a reliable aeroplane, but the Royal Navy wanted an aircraft with better performance. The result was the Fairey Firefly. Like the Fulmar, the Firefly was a rather large carrier-borne two-seater, with good range. It was well-armed with four 20-mm cannons in the wings and was surprisingly manoeuvrable for such a large aeroplane. It served in the Second World War in the Pacific, and was used in the Korean War by the Royal Navy.

1/72 Scale Special Hobby Fairey Firefly TT.4 by Bill Gilman
I've always loved the yellow and black stripes on the underside of target tugs, and since I'm also a big fan of the Fairey Firefly, this was an ideal project. To make the model more interesting, I decided to fold the wings and add extra detail. Since folded wings are not a feature of the kit, a bit of conversion and scratchbuilding was in order. That's part of the allure of scale modelling—improving on what's in the kit to make it uniquely your own.

  The Special Hobby kit is 'multimedia' right out of the box and has nicely cast resin components and a photoetched fret. Before starting, however, I did a lot of

With a little extra work, Special Hobby's 1/72 scale Firefly TT.4 is transformed into a display case showstopper. (*Bill Gilman*)

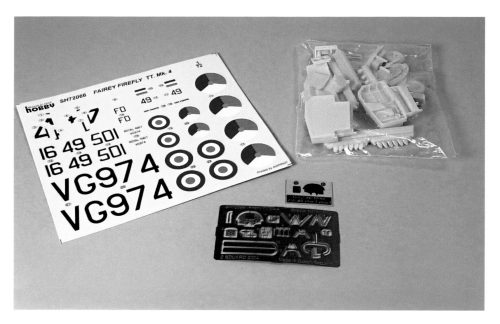

The kit includes nicely cast resin parts and photoetched details. A bit of conversion and scratchbuilding will kick it up a notch or two. (*Bill Gilman*)

internet research to acquire a large number of reference photos showing the folding wing mechanism. Those of you who are familiar with Fairey Aviation's folding wing designs know that they can be, shall we say, a bit unusual. Good reference material is essential!

The Build

As is typically the case, the build starts with the cockpit. Special Hobby provide most of the cockpit components in resin, providing much more detail than would be possible with injected styrene. When sawing through the pour blocks, the thinner the razor saw blade the better. The blade I use is probably as thick as you want to go. (I've asked the wife for a new, thinner one, but instead I got a list of chores to do in the garden. Go figure.)

It's easy to start cutting and zip right on through, but you incur the risk of cutting at an angle, thereby slicing into the part, or otherwise damaging the piece. If you have any kind of clamping jig that can hold the part 'square' so you can saw true, that's ideal. Here is the trick I use: I make a small starter cut all around the part. For this seat, it's easy as it's approximately square. I carefully saw completely through, with the starter cuts helping to guide the saw and keep it straight. Always monitor your progress to keep on track for a good, clean separation. It's not a perfect technique, but it seems to work for me.

Sometimes, you have to sand the entire pour block off as the part is cast lying on top of it. A case in point here is the rear bulkhead with its lightening holes. This part is small enough to use a typical sanding stick, as shown. When parts get larger than this, tape a large piece of sandpaper to a flat surface and use that. Holding onto the part can sometimes be difficult, especially since you want the sanded surface to be true and flat. Clamping tweezers can help in such a case. For this part, it's fun to watch the lightening holes magically appear as you sand. When that happens, you know you've sanded enough!

Cockpits on the TT.4 were black, which creates a bit of a conundrum for the modeller. How to paint and not end up with a 'coal hole' where all the details disappear in the darkness? Here is what I did: The overall colour is Tamiya NATO Black; highlights are in Extra Dark Sea Grey; controls are grey and silver; and I applied a black wash. What? A black wash on a black cockpit? It works because NATO Black is really a very dark grey, and the black wash shows up nicely and adds shadows to increase the contrast. Some folks use a medium grey wash on top of black, but to me that just looks odd.

The cockpit was completed without any difficulties and added to the fuselage along with some nice resin exhausts. The fuselage was then buttoned up. Here I discovered a major error: Special Hobby did not include the characteristic carburettor intake below the spinner. My only choice was to 'scab' one on with sheet styrene. A bit of trial and error determined the final shape of the piece, while making sure that the opening up front matched the photographs. After the styrene was in place, it was faired into the fuselage using spot glazing putty.

There was nowhere to hide now—I had to tackle the folding wings. First, using my reference photos, I determined the exact lines to cut along. Luckily, these were all existing

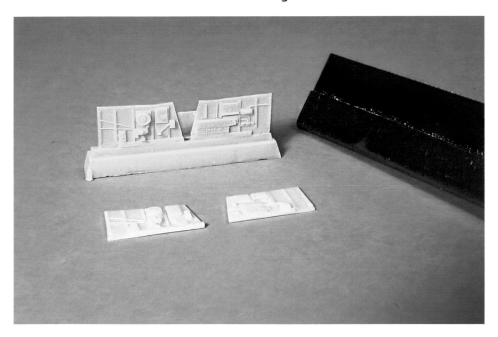

Removing resin parts from their pour blocks requires the right tools but is not difficult. (*Bill Gilman*)

Sanding the entire pour block away allows the lightening holes to appear as if by magic. (*Bill Gilman*)

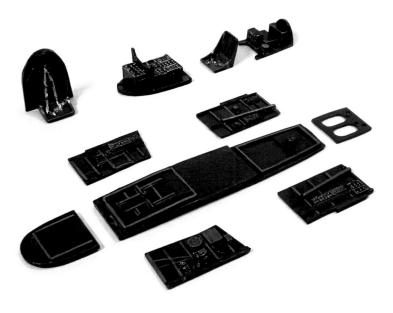

Using dark greys instead of black ensures your cockpit doesn't become a 'coal hole'. (*Bill Gilman*)

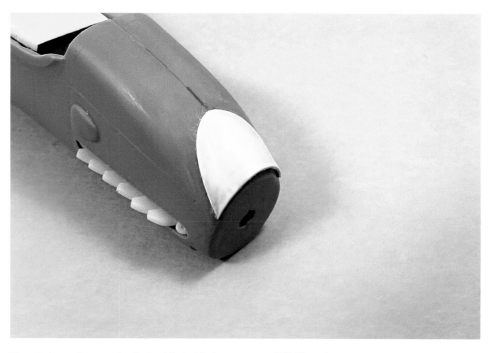

The missing carburettor intake is added with sheet styrene. (*Bill Gilman*)

panel lines, but unluckily, this would not be a simple straight cut. I decided the best way to achieve these cuts was to use a Tamiya (Olfa) Panel Line Scriber and continue to scribe over the lines until I had broken through the plastic completely. It sounds crazy, but it allowed me to have all those right-angle corners along the cut without damaging either portion of the wing. When all was said and done (and it took a while), I was left with what's pictured below.

Next, I added the resin wheel wells to the underside fuselage, only to find that the outboard portions extended beyond the wing fold, which they do not do in real life. I had no choice but to cut off the offending portion, and repair with some sheet styrene.

Having made all the cuts, I then had to scratchbuild the area underneath the wing root fairings, which was now exposed. Back to the reference photos, and I was able to put together a reasonable facsimile using styrene sheet and solder wire.

With the wings folded, the inner structural details are visible, and based on the reference photos, there are a lot of them. Since this was 1/72 scale, it was impractical to do them all, so I chose what I felt would make for a good replica. Then it was back to the styrene stock and wire, and a few iterations later I was happy. Lightening holes were made with a punch and die set, along with the ubiquitous No. 11 blade. I chose to model the wing-locking lever (the irregularly shaped object at the front of the inboard wing section) stowed and locked. Since they are delicate, I planned to add some of the photoetched details later to avoid knocking them off into the ether.

Special Hobby provide the basic shapes for the gear doors, but they are simply flat pieces of styrene—in other words, no extra structural detail. I decided to recreate the large fuselage door with sheet styrene so I could make the recessed areas. I also decided to use small diameter wire to create the stiffeners on the doors attached to the leg. In the photo on the left we have the Special Hobby parts, and on the right, my feeble attempt at adding some interest. I was confident that, once it was painted and given a light wash, it would do the trick.

At this point the model was primed with Alclad Grey, and some minor touch-ups were affected. I then sprayed the underside with Testors Yellow, and after that had cured, I masked off the silver areas and sprayed Alclad High Speed Silver to replicate the aluminium paint. Unfortunately, some of the yellow pulled up when I removed the tape, necessitating an unexpected repair job. The wheel wells and landing gear struts were painted to match my references.

Target tugs are typically equipped with diagonal black stripes on the underside, and these needed to be painted onto the model. Steve Long from the Camden Museum of Aviation in Australia was kind enough to provide copies of the original painting specifications and drawings, and these were very helpful in masking the stripes. I used Gunze Tyre Black instead of 'normal' black as I wanted something more like a very dark grey. Of course, the stripes will continue onto the lower surface of the wings.

After the basic painting of the fuselage was finished, I used one of my favourites, Gunze Smoke Grey, to add a bit of weathering. The paint was highly thinned (around 80 parts thinner to 20 parts paint) and applied in random areas in a light mist using the smallest needle in my airbrush. I find this quite effective on an aluminium finish such as this.

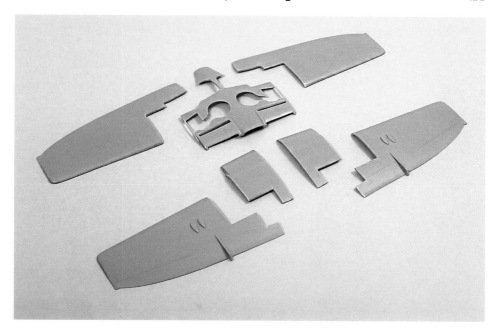

A panel line scriber makes it easy to cut all these right-angled corners. (*Bill Gilman*)

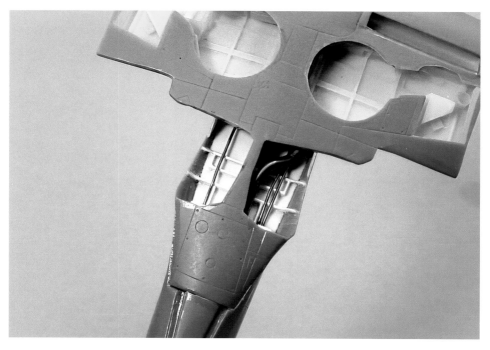

Sheet styrene and solder wire are used to create internal and structural details—reference photos are your best friends! (*Bill Gilman*)

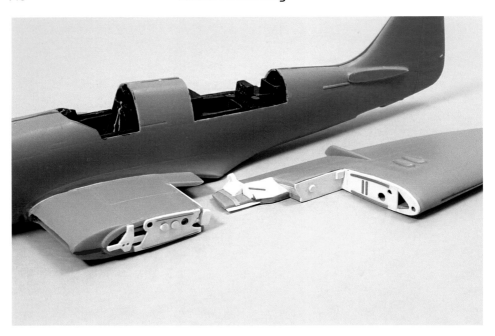

Building the internal wing details with sheet styrene, wire, and tape. A punch and die set make quick work of small holes and bosses. (*Bill Gilman*)

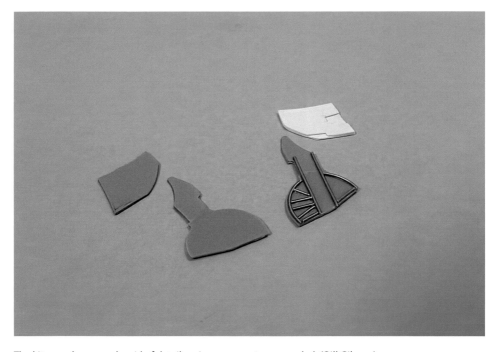

The kit gear doors are devoid of detail, so improvements are needed. (*Bill Gilman*)

There are also flaps/covers that hinge at the forward edge of the lower radiator openings, and these seem to be open in most of the pictures. Special Hobby included these with the kit, but I made new ones out of thinner card stock to be added later on.

A prominent feature on the underside, also not part of the kit, is the target banner chute, positioned right between the tines of the arresting hook. It's somewhat of a D-shaped oval, and I added this with sheet styrene that I formed around an old paintbrush handle. Speaking of the arresting hook, I decided to scratchbuild one instead of using the parts from the kit. I planned to add it at the end of the build along with the other fiddly bits.

Also missing from the kit are the vanes inside of the radiator intakes. I planned to make these out of styrene stock as well, and paint them before sliding them in. They have to be yellow on the bottom half and aluminium on the top, and it is much easier to paint them before assembly.

An easy way to improve the model was to add navigation and landing lights. Accordingly, notches were cut out of the wings and painted aluminium, representing the colour of the interior structure. Next, some oversized clear plastic 'bits' were superglued in place. Of course, oversized bits are used in anticipation of sanding, shaping, and polishing. In this case, the clear plastic bits were cut out of some disposable cutlery—you never know where you might find materials for detailing your model!

Prior to attaching the clear bits for the navigation lights, I drilled small holes to represent the filaments, and filled the holes with Gunze Clear Red and Clear Green respectively (for port and starboard lights). Photoetched parts for the landing light came from Marabu Designs, and these were glued to the wing prior to the clear bit going on.

To finish the job, sanding sticks of progressively finer grades were used to shape the clear bits into the desired form of the lenses. Various Micro-Mesh pads polished them up nicely.

The wings were then painted with the same colours as the fuselage. The black stripes on the underside of the wings were not quite as dramatic as I had expected—the official painting diagram shows that the stripes did not extend over any control surfaces and a yellow background was to remain in the area where the codes are applied (for visibility). It meant quite a bit of masking for not a lot of stripes!

At this time, I also painted the drop tanks and winch. The latter has two windows on it according to reference photos. I took the easy way out and represented these with decals. The small propeller blades on the front of the winch, made from photoetch, really look the part, but be careful to mount them at the correct angle. Again, reference photos are your best friends. The port drop tank has a black anti-glare patch to minimise reflection from the landing light.

One of my favourite modelling activities is the application of the decals. I even like those modern planes with a myriad of stencils, but the markings for this kit are pretty basic and did not take long to apply. The tyres were painted and a light wash was applied prior to adding them to the landing gear. Instead of the kit tyres, I used resin aftermarket parts from Barracuda as I felt the tread pattern was better.

I added catapult hooks to the lower side of the forward fuselage (near the inner edge of the radiator opening), and I also added the lower radiator flaps, made from sheet

The characteristic target tug stripes were painted using official Fleet Air Arm documentation as a guide. (*Bill Gilman*)

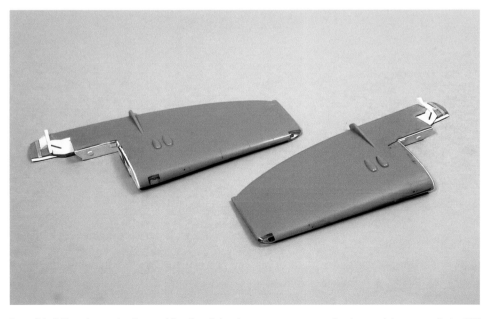

Scratchbuilding the navigation and landing lights is an easy way to make the model more realistic. (*Bill Gilman*)

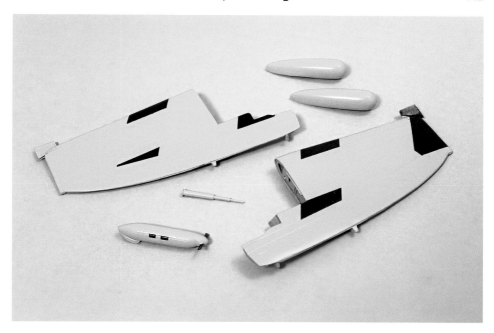

With underwing codes and drop tanks, there's not much room for stripes. (*Bill Gilman*)

Random application of highly thinned Smoke Grey gives the aluminium finish that 'lived-in' look. (*Bill Gilman*)

styrene, staging them in a partially open position. The arresting hook and tailwheel doors were added in the back, and all the canopy masking was removed. Sections of the under-wing codes were applied to the gear doors (thankfully Special Hobby provided these pre-cut to the right shape), and the doors were then added to the model.

CRUNCH TIME

Now it was time for the 20 per cent of the build that takes 80 per cent of the time—the fiddly bits. Special Hobby provide a nicely done photoetched fret that includes the bracketry for the winch pod and spool, and these are very fiddly indeed. To ensure a good bond, I drilled 0.1-mm holes into the fuselage as attachment points. Although the brackets look rather spindly, the photoetch is strong enough to support the winch and the scale fidelity of the photoetched parts is quite good, especially for 1/72 scale.

The radiator intakes are rather prominent, and a bit of extra detail will create a more realistic representation. A photoetched mesh was added to the front of the radiators, followed by the vanes, which were made from sheet styrene and painted as described previously.

The Firefly TT.4 has a variety of guards to prevent the target line and drogue from getting accidentally tangled in the tail control surfaces and tailwheel. Special Hobby give you the guard for the tailwheel, but those for the tailplanes and elevators have to be scratchbuilt.

Before the wings can be added to the fuselage, I decided that I should add the wing fold latch pin fittings, as they are an important part of the mechanism. When the wing is spread, the lock lever is pushed into the locked position, which pushes the four latch pins into the fittings. The fittings are small, but I had some extra photoetched parts that worked nicely. As I said before, you never know where you might find the materials you need—in this case, the parts came from a 1/24 scale photoetched fret of NASCAR windshield clips. (Please do not ask why I had one of these.) As you can imagine, these were also rather fiddly. Once they were in place on the inboard section of the outer wings, they really added to the realistic look of the model.

Now it was time to add the wings. After studying the reference photos, I gave up on my original idea of a working hinge. I may build 1/72 scale airplanes, but I'm not crazy (yet)! Instead, I quickly came to the realisation that I would need to have a jig to position the wings at the correct angles. I knew the join had to be strong, so I used a short piece of brass tubing as a pin between the inner and outer wing sections. This pin was positioned at the hinge location, and I built two jigs from my grandson's construction blocks. I measured the wing angles from photographs and tested everything beforehand. Sliding the jig along the bottom edge of the wing adjusted how far above the horizontal tailplane the end of the wing would be, and the angle of the tilted block adjusted the splay of the wings (when folded, the top of the wing splays out relative to the bottom of the wing). Each jig also had a slot formed between the blocks in which the wing sat, and another slot for clearance of the drop tanks.

I took photos of the setup, measured the angles, and made slight adjustments to the jig. When I was satisfied the angles were right, I mixed up some epoxy adhesive, glued the wings on, and left things overnight to cure.

The winch attachment posts may look fiddly, but they really look the part in 1/72 scale. (*Bill Gilman*)

The tailwheel guard, arresting hook, and spool dress up the underside of this target tug. (*Bill Gilman*)

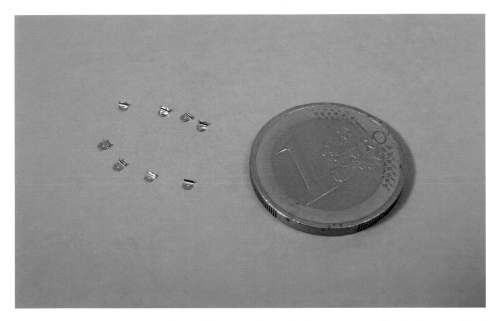

It doesn't matter where they come from—these tiny, photoetched parts are just what the doctor ordered. (*Bill Gilman*)

They are the perfect size to replicate the wing fold latch pin fittings. (*Bill Gilman*)

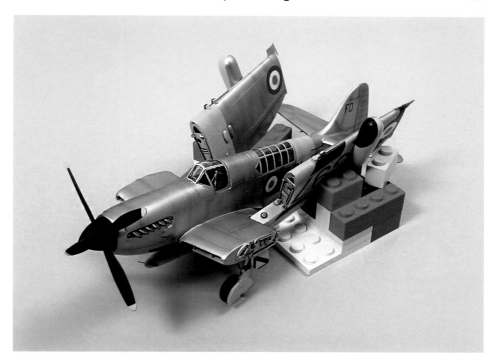

Relive your youth and put those construction blocks to good use. (*Bill Gilman*)

The remaining bits were then added. The guards for the elevators (the rounded brackets at the tip of the tailplane) were made with copper wire and the cables from Nitinol wire. The latter is a 'shape memory alloy' that I often use instead of stretched sprue. The wire I use is 0.2 mm in diameter, but is straight and rigid with minimal sagging for this application. I simply cut it to the correct length and position it on the model.

The wing jury struts were made from styrene rod, and the antennae were a combination of kit parts, photoetch, and Nitinol wire. The kit provides photoetched flare shields for the exhaust, and the final touch was the scratchbuilt mirror/air inlet on top of the windscreen and the mirror on the top of the port wing.

So, the Firefly target tug adventure comes to a close. A little extra work, conversion of the kit's wings, and some extra detail made for a satisfying project and a nice addition to the display case. Hopefully you've picked up a few ideas and have seen how some relatively simple modifications to a basic kit can really enhance the model. Give it a try on your next project!

The finished model really benefits from the modifications and extra detail. (*Bill Gilman*)

The basic short-run kit is significantly enhanced with a few simple modifications and some extra details. Coming at you! (*Bill Gilman*)

Conclusion

Well, there you have it—an indication of what can be achieved with some effort, patience, and a bit of modelling skill. If you find the extraordinary modelling skill displayed in the preceding pages a bit daunting, fear not. Although most modellers (including myself) will never achieve the mastery displayed by the experts in this book, the same enhancing techniques can still be used by modellers of average ability. Even if you never attempt a scratchbuilt, resin, or vacuform kit, the techniques involved in building these models can also be applied to mainstream injection-moulded polystyrene kits. It is my sincere hope that this book will help those modellers who have outgrown the 'average' and wish to achieve a little more with their models. As mentioned in the introduction, it will hopefully encourage modellers to attempt some ambitious subjects, more ambitious than they might otherwise have tried. So, give it a try, and always remember that your model is being made for you; if you are satisfied with it, then you have achieved your goal.

Internet Resources

Britmodeller.com—several of the models which appear in this book made their first appearance on this website, which I have found to be an excellent modelling website, full of outstanding models and modellers. Even a few of my modest creations have appeared on this site (but do not hold that against it!).

Index

Numbers in italics are picture references.

ALSO AVAILABLE

FIRST WORLD WAR AIRCRAFT
IN SCALE
Scratchbuilding in 1/144 Scale